Be A Leader, Not A Boss

John P. Nesgoda III

Copyright © 2020 John Paul Nesgoda III

All rights reserved. This book or any portion thereof may not be reproduced or used in any manner whatsoever without the expressed written permission of the publisher except for the use of brief quotations in a book review.

Contents

Acknowledgments 4

Introduction 5

SECTION ONE
DEFINING A LEADER 7

1. Leadership Qualities 8
2. Servant Leadership 24
3. Micromanaging 28
4. Emotional Intelligence 34

SECTION TWO
BEST PRACTICES 44

5. Communication 45
6. Time Management 56
7. Meetings 62

SECTION THREE
EMPLOYEE INTERACTION 68

8. Hiring / Interviewing 69
9. Evaluating Team Members 76
10. Team Management 83
11. Managing Difficult Employees 96
12. Dealing with Employee Conflict 103
13. Dealing with Toxic Environment 110
14. Written Corrections 117
15. Firing an Employee 122
16. Recognition 127

17. Managing Generations   132

SECTION FOUR
UNDERSTAND YOUR ROLE   **141**

18. Implementing Change   142
19. Project Management   158
20. Delegation   166
21. Negotiations   175
22. Networking   182
23. Office Politics   188
24. Next Steps   192

Conclusion   197
Index   198

Acknowledgments

I want to acknowledge all of my Team Members, Supervisors, Managers, and Directors that I have worked with over the years. You have provided insight, inspiration, and direction; you have been my colleagues, peers, friends, and mentors throughout my journey.

To my family, for your understanding and support, you have provided me over the years. For having to deal with all the late-night conference calls, traveling on business, missed dinners, and family events. You have always stood by my side.

I would also like to acknowledge all of the managers and leaders who are reading this book. You are the ones that are making a positive difference every day for your teams, their families, and your organization.

Introduction

Being a leader isn't just about being the boss. As a leader, you need to ensure you are there for your team and not just there to hand out orders. Some of the worst managers were just as insightful as some of the best ones I have had. If you worked in any business or corporate environment, you would most likely encounter the good, the bad, and the ugly at one point or another.

A little bit about myself, I have been in leadership positions in one form or fashion since 2004. I have worked in all types of environments, from small companies to large international organizations. I have worked in some of the most diverse cities in the world. It does not matter what setting in which you work. This material will show how to be a successful leader regardless of the experience you have in a management role.

Being a leader can be one of the most challenging and rewarding roles in any environment. A leader is crucial to any work environment and can take an excellent work environment and turn it into a toxic one or take a lousy work environment into a positive, enjoyable one.

You have taken the first step in becoming a successful modern-day leader, and this material will cover areas you should focus on and things you should avoid. Will, there are some things that you should avoid doing, there are plenty of common-sense best practices you should be doing. This material will help you create an environment for your team that is engaged, productive, and happy.

"Leadership and learning are indispensable to each other."

- *John F. Kennedy*

SECTION ONE

DEFINING A LEADER

Leadership (noun) lead·er·ship - The action of leading a group of people or an organization. "different styles of leadership"

Synonyms: guidance, direction, control, management, superintendence, supervision; guidance, direction, control, management, superintendence, supervision, directorship, governorship, governance, administration, captaincy, control, ascendancy, supremacy, rule, command, power, dominion, influence

1
Leadership Qualities

"If your actions inspire others to dream more, learn more, do more and become more, you are a leader."

- *John Quincy Adams*

IF YOU HAD TO DEFINE A GREAT LEADER, what are some areas would they excel? Ultimately, a great leader creates a positive environment and nurtures its employees. A great leader has a clear vision, is courageous, has integrity, is honest, and shows humility and has a clear focus. He or she is a strategic planner and believes in teamwork.

Leaders do not exist to order employees around. A leader needs to trust your employees to perform their tasks professionally and independently. Spending time with each employee to get to know the individual and how they fit on your team will help build that trust.

Managers who show great leadership qualities can accomplish amazing things with their teams. Certain leadership qualities not only drive companies but also continuously inspire teams.

While managers still have authority, the modern manager must understand that empowerment creates a culture of ownership, responsibility, and accountability. Managers must understand how to properly motivate their employees because managers in today's business world cannot do everything themselves. Understanding how to delegate effectively and how to communicate the organizational goals and objectives effectively will allow today's manager to be more successful.

The terms manager and leader are often used interchangeably, but it is essential to understand the difference between the two. Management is about getting things done through others, while leadership is about influencing and inspiring people to work towards a common goal. This is important because managers are often called upon to be leaders within their organizations.

Big Five Personality Traits

While there are several different models to categorize the characteristics of a leader, the "Big Five" model is the most widely excepted. The traits are openness, conscientiousness, extraversion agreeableness, and neuroticism. Several of the Big Five personality traits have been related to leadership emergence and effectiveness.

There are many tests you can take online to see how you score in each of the categories. Keep in mind that personality tests can sometimes help you better understand yourself to better one's self. They cannot completely define who you are as a person or describe you fully even if they get some things right.

Openness

Openness is a strong predictor of who will become and succeed as a leader. It means you are original, imaginative, daring, you have broad interests and you generally prefer variety over fixed routines.

People high in openness seem to thrive in situations that require flexibility and learning new things. Individuals who have this trait are more likely to be drawn to jobs with a creative component.

Conscientiousness

Conscientiousness is the best predictor of both personal and professional success. It's also the strongest predictor of leadership in different contexts, including business, government, and school. It means you are hardworking ambitious, energetic, and you like planning things. Conscientiousness, more so than the other Big Five personality traits, is related to leader emergence and effectiveness.

Conscientiousness is the one personality trait that uniformly predicts how high a person's performance will be across a variety of occupations and jobs. The ability of those high in conscientiousness to be reliable and rational decision-makers has advantages on and off the job.

Extraversion

Extroversion is another strong predictor of who will become a leader — though psychologists are increasingly discovering that introverts can do just as well in leadership roles. It means you are sociable, fun-loving, affectionate, friendly, talkative, and you pull your energy from social activities. Out of all the personality traits, extraversion has the strongest relationship with both leader emergence and leader effectiveness. This is not to say that all effective leaders are extraverts, but you are more likely to find extraverts in leadership positions.

Interacting with others and being social energizes extraverts, whereas similar levels of stimulation and interactions may be viewed as draining to someone who is an introvert. One of the established findings is that extraverts tend to be effective in jobs involving sales.

Agreeableness

Agreeable people tend to be happier, possibly because they try to avoid negative experiences. On the other hand, disagreeable people may be more likely to succeed at work because they're better at getting their ideas heard. It means you are tolerant, sensitive, trusting, kind, and warm.

People who are high in agreeableness are likable people and get along with others. Not surprisingly, agreeable people help others at work consistently; this helping behavior does not depend on their good mood. They are also less likely to retaliate when other people mistreat them.

Being agreeable may reflect their ability to show empathy and to give people the benefit of the doubt. Agreeable people may be a valuable addition to their teams and maybe effective leaders because they create a positive environment when they are in leadership positions. They are regarded as highly ethical leaders by their subordinates.

Neuroticism

Neuroticism is also sometimes called Emotional Stability. This dimension relates to one's emotional stability and degree of negative emotions. Neurotic people tend to react to perceived threats and stressful situations. It means you worry a lot, and you're moody, irritable temperamental and sometimes anxious.

It is perhaps the only Big Five dimension were scoring high is undesirable. People that score high in neuroticism experience several problems at work, mostly because of their difficulties with handling stress. Neurotic people tend to experience anger when confronted with the daily hassles of their work, including time pressure and red tape, and they respond to this daily stress by drinking after hours.

Good Leadership Qualities

Accountability

Being a good leader also means being accountable, not only for yourself but for your team as well. Take the good with the bad; we all have setbacks, use them as learning experiences to grow. Accountable leaders do not blame others when things go wrong and take responsibility and act to improve the situation.

While holding themselves accountable is an important part of being a leader it is also equally important to hold others accountable when concerns or deficiencies are identified. By not holding members on your team accountable for issues it can have a negative impact on those that are doing their jobs properly.

The building of a trusting relationship takes time, it is not a one-time event. While we live in a society that is very unforgiving of mistakes, in order to build trust within an organization, it is more important to be authentic and human than it is to be perfect. When a mistake is made by a leader, it should be owned and acknowledged. Sometimes that acknowledgment needs to be made public; sometimes it needs to be private.

Delegation and Empowerment

It is essential to learn how to delegate. Not all tasks need to be handled by you; most new employees in a leadership role struggle with this. Learning to delegate is one of the hardest things to do, especially when you know you can do it effectively.

It is also crucial to learn how to delegate because when you do, you empower the employee to make their own decisions to complete the task. Stand behind their choices and encourage them and coach when needed.

Empowerment is the process of enabling or authorizing an individual to think, behave, take action, and control work and decision making in autonomous ways.

Honesty

Influential leaders treat people the way they want to be treated as they are extremely ethical and believe that honesty, effort, and reliability form the foundation of success. They embody these values so overtly that no employee doubts their integrity for a minute. They share information openly.

It is essential to share information openly. However, some topics it is difficult to be transparent. If there is the elephant in the room that they would like to talk about, but can't, tell them you can't but will when the time is right. Honesty creates trust, and there are far few things more important than building trust between yourself and your team.

Empathetic

Empathy is defined as the ability to understand one's perspective and feelings and experiences. You will not be able to build a team or nurture a new generation of leaders with it as you will not be able to inspire others or create loyalty.

It is essential to listen and truly listen to your people. There are usually hidden emotions behind what the employee is saying. You must be present, put the phone down and give the employee your full attention.

Don't interrupt the employee, and give them time to get their message out. Don't rush to give advice or change the subject. Take a personal interest in people, ask them about what is going on in their lives. Talk to them about their hobbies, families, etc.

Discipline / Self-control

Maintaining self-control and emotional balance is a critical area that all needs must focus on as it maximizes performance, especially when dealing with adversity. As a leader, you are more likely to inspire your team instead of being abusive or having to micromanage them

Integrity

Research has also shown that people who are competent as leaders tend to have a moral compass and demonstrate honesty and integrity. Leaders whose integrity is questioned lose their trustworthiness, and they hurt their company's business along the way.

Understand Your Mission and Vision

Most companies have a mission statement, which is defined as a formal summary of the aims and values of a company, organization, or individual. Whether your focus is on doing what is right for your customers or caring for a patient, the why is essential to your company, and it should be relevant to you and your team.

Leaders will need to carry out the planning facet by defining the mission and vision. Developing a strategy to carry out the mission and vision and establishing goals and objectives to indicate how successful the strategy is. Leaders will develop the organizing facet by adequately designing and structuring the organization to achieve organizational goals and objectives and to cultivate an organizational culture that inspires and motivates employees.

By understanding your Mission Statement and the "Why" behind it creates a driving culture in your team. What do Steve Jobs (Apple), and Jeff Bezos (Amazon) have in common? A universal message and mission, and by understanding that they drove their companies to new levels. A mission statement that is taken seriously and widely communicated may provide insights into the corporate culture.

A vision statement, in contrast, is a future-oriented declaration of the organization's purpose and aspirations. In many ways, you can say that the mission statement lays out the organization's "purpose for being," and the vision statement then says, "based on that purpose, this is what we want to become."

A casual tour of a business or organization website will expose you to the range of forms that mission and vision statements can take. Mission statements answer the questions of "Who are we?" and "What does our organization value?" Vision statements typically take the form of relatively brief, future-oriented statements—vision statements answer the question "Where is this organization going?"

The Six Emotional Leadership Styles

Daniel Goleman, Richard Boyatzis, and Annie McKee detailed their Six Emotional Leadership Styles theory in their 2002 book, "Primal Leadership." The approach highlights the strengths and weaknesses of six common styles – Visionary, Coaching, Affiliative, Democratic, Pacesetting, and Commanding. It also shows how each form can affect the emotions of your team members.

It is essential to keep in mind that it is rare for any leader to have just one leadership style. Most leaders will have two or more leadership styles that shine through.

Coercive

The coercive style seeks immediate compliance from employees. As a style that can be linked to that of a dictatorship, it can be summed up with, "Do what I tell you." This type of leader demands immediate compliance.

Pacesetting

Similar to the coercive style, the pacesetting style should be used sparingly. It is also known as the "do as I do, now" style. This type of leader expects excellence and self-direction.

Visionary

In the authoritative style, visionary leaders take a "firm but fair" approach that mobilizes members toward a specific goal. This leader mobilizes their people toward a shared vision.

Democratic

The democratic style can be summed up with the question "What do you think?" Focused on getting feedback, leaders can receive valuable ideas and confirmation while building an environment of trust, commitment, and respect. This type of leader builds consensus through participation.

Affiliative

In this "people come first" style, an affiliative leader praises and nurtures members to cultivate a sense of belonging in an organization. This type of leader creates emotional bonds and harmony.

Coaching

Some leaders can maximize their workers' effectiveness by acting as a coach instead of a traditional boss. In the "try this" model, leaders that focus on the strengths and weaknesses of an employee to improve and encourage him or her along the way. This type of leader develops people for the future.

The Five Major Leadership Styles

Before the list of "Six Emotional Leadership Styles," there was a definitive list of five major leadership styles. This list is a combination of leadership styles from that date back to the 1930s to more modern times.

Regardless of the era, they come from, the styles transcend the passage of time and still reflect styles of leadership that can be incorporated into the six emotional leadership styles. Which when you tie to the two together paints a good picture of your overall leadership style.

1. **Bureaucratic leadership**, whose leaders focus on following every rule.

2. **Laissez-faire leadership** is a leadership style that gives their team members a lot of freedom in how the work is accomplished and how their deadlines are set.

3. **Charismatic leadership**, in which leaders inspire enthusiasm in their teams and are energetic in motivating others to move forward.

4. **Servant leadership**, whose leaders focus on meeting the needs of the team.

5. **Transactional leadership**, in which leaders inspire by expecting the best from everyone and themselves.

Transformational Leadership

Transformational leadership theories believe that people are motivated by the task that must be performed. The more structured an organization is, the greater the success. People give their all to the organization which can be their primary need and they will place their individual interests second. Transformational leaders inspire followers to perform beyond expectations by developing, intellectually stimulating, and inspiring followers to transcend their own self-interests for a higher collective purpose, mission, or vision.

Pro's

- Transformational leadership theories emphasize the task and organizational integrity and this helps focus one's attention to more appropriately defining a task.
- The transformational theories emphasize cooperation, ethics and community in addition to the higher human values.
- Long-range goals are emphasized which leads to increasing the survivability of a system.
- It has been showed in studies, such as in gaming theory, that cooperation, as opposed to competition, is more successful in achieving goals.
- Transformational leadership theories are adaptive and can be tailored to support the fulfillment of the most pressing of needs in people.
- There is greater stability of a leader's position, as there is greater support by those who are being led.
- Transformational leadership theories can bring harmony to a situation that could otherwise be exacerbated by a quarrelsome organization.
- If one has an educated population, transformational leadership theories are more likely to work.

Con's

- Even if everyone is motivated to do a task it does not assure a successful completion of that task. Over-enthusiasm for the leader may cloud the group's judgment as to whether the objectives of an organization are realistic.
- There can be over-dependence upon the leader.
- Members of the organization may resent that their ability to act as individuals has been restricted.
- People have different personalities, and some may be more ambitious than others may, with the latter feeling as if they are being pushed beyond their capacities.
- Some individuals may work better as individuals as opposed to collaborating in a team environment.
- There may be cases when it is difficult to assess whether there is cooperation or mere conformity. People may want simply to "go along to get along".
- There is the danger of the presence of personality cults, where a leader is so revered that s/he is only the personality that drives activity.
- The enormity of a task and a fractious or highly competitive environment may compromise the ability of a leader, applying the concepts of transformational leadership theories, to gain consensus.

What People Look for in Their Leaders

On the next couple of pages, you will see the Characteristics of Admired Leaders (CAL) table. Over one-hundred thousand people around the globe have responded to the CAL checklist. The survey results have been remarkable in their consistency over the years. There are some essential "character tests" individuals must pass before others are willing to grant them the designation leader.

While every characteristic receives votes, meaning that each is important to some people. What is most evident and striking is that for over three decades, there are only four qualities that have always received more than 60 percent of the votes (except for Inspiring in 1987, which was valued by 58 percent at that time). Despite all the dramatic changes in the world, what people most look for in a leader has been amazingly stable.

Percentage of Respondents Selecting Each Characteristic Over Time Periods*

Characteristic	1987	1995	2002	2007	2012	2017
Honest	83	88	88	89	89	84
Competent	67	63	66	68	69	66
Inspiring	58	68	65	69	69	66
Forward-Looking	62	75	71	71	71	62
Intelligent	43	40	47	48	45	47
Broad-minded	37	40	40	35	38	40
Dependable	33	32	33	34	35	39
Supportive	32	41	35	35	35	37
Fair-minded	40	49	42	39	37	35
Straightforward	34	33	34	36	32	32
Cooperative	25	28	28	25	27	31
Ambitious	21	13	17	16	21	28
Caring	26	23	20	22	21	23
Determined	17	17	23	25	26	22
Courageous	27	29	20	25	22	22
Loyal	11	11	14	18	19	18
Imaginative	34	28	23	17	16	17
Mature	23	13	21	5	14	17
Self-Controlled	13	5	8	10	11	10
Independent	10	5	6	4	5	5

* Note: Since we asked people to select seven characteristics, the totals add up to more than 100 percent.

For the majority of people to follow someone willingly, they want a leader who they believe is:

1. Honest
2. Competent
3. Inspiring
4. Forward-looking

In addition, these same four characteristics rank consistently at the top across different countries as shown by the data in the table below. It was also found that the ranking doesn't significantly vary across cultures, ethnicities, organizational functions and hierarchies, genders, levels of education, and age groups.

Country	Honest	Forward-looking	Inspiring	Competent
United States	1	2	3	4
Australia	1	2	3	4
Brazil	1	2	4	3
Canada	1*	1*	3	4
China	3	2	1	4
Japan	1*	1*	4	3
Korea	1*	1*	4	3
Malaysia	1	2	4	3
Mexico	1	2	3	4
Scandinavia	3	2	1	4
Singapore	4	2*	1	2*
Turkey	3	1	2	4
United Arab Emirates	1	2	3	4

* Indicates a tie in the rank order.

Things to Avoid

Behind Closed Doors

Do not condemn someone within the company in public. This will generally demoralize the employee and lower their self-esteem. In the end, it will hurt the efficiency and productivity of the employee.

Make Time

Not making time for your team. It is easy for any leader to focus on all of the tasks they have every day. Make sure you are spending some time or least checking in with your team a few times a day.

Don't Be Too Removed

Unless you are leading a project, being too hands off on any project is a bad thing. While delegating is an integral part of being a leader avoid and micromanaging is a bad thing, you need to find the right balance.

Move On

Misunderstanding your role is a common mistake with most new leaders. Once you move into a leadership role, your responsibilities are very different from those you had before.

Listen To Your Employees

You would think this is a no-brainer but if you look at other managers within your own landscape and pay close attention this is usually a chronic issue in most organizations. Not listening to your employees as often as possible is a common mistake made by managers. By listening to them often you are building loyalty and trust.

Not Being Visible

One of the critical things a leader must do daily is to be visible to your team. It is crucial to reach out to your employees every day. The encounters do not need to be formal, and it could just be as simple as seeing how their day is going.

Being visible lets your team know that you are there for them, and you acknowledge them. It will keep the morale high through the connections that you are making with them.

Don't Use Fear as A Leadership Tool

A leader-constituent relationship characterized by fear and distrust will never produce anything of lasting value. A relationship characterized by mutual respect and confidence will overcome the greatest adversities and leave a legacy of significance.

2
Servant Leadership

"A leader is best when people barely know he exists when his work is done, his aim fulfilled, they will say: we did it ourselves."

- Lao Tzu

THE TERM "SERVANT LEADERSHIP" was first coined by Robert Greenleaf in 1970. Traditional leadership generally involves the exercise of power by one at the "top of the pyramid." By comparison, the servant-leader shares power puts the needs of others first and helps people develop and perform as highly as possible.

The servant-leader is servant first… It begins with the natural feeling that one wants to serve, to serve first. Then conscious choice brings one to aspire to lead. That person is sharply different from one who is leader first, perhaps because of the need to assuage an unusual power drive or to acquire material possessions…The leader-first and the servant-first are two extreme types. Between them there are shadings and blends that are part of the infinite variety of human nature.

Servant leadership turns the power pyramid upside down, which puts the typically low-level employees at the top of the pyramid;

instead of the people working to serve the leader, the leader exists to help the people.

This model can be a difficult transition for most managers who are used to putting their needs first and are usually driven by success. You must genuinely want to help your employees for this model to be successful. There is nothing more gratifying than to help develop your employees to achieve their goals. Regardless of the organization you work for this leadership style is useful, and you can make significant changes in the organization.

Nine Qualities of a Servant Leader

1. **Values Others Opinions** - A servant leader values everyone's opinions and their contributions.

2. **Cultivates an Environment of Trust** – A Servant leader does not promote gossiping and does not promote an environment that accepts that.

3. **Develops Leaders** – A servant leader understands the importance of developing others. It is a matter of leading by example and teaching others. Sometimes the leader must not always lead, but instead give up power to allow others to lead so others can learn.

4. **Helps people with life issues** – There is no question that focusing on business is a top priority when working with your employees. However, a servant leader will help their employees with some life issues, such as certain family situations, and seeking to help them with find education for debt concerns.

5. **Encourages Employees** - The corner stone of any servant leader is <u>encouragement</u>. A servant leader also understands to get involved with employees when working on issues. The servant leader will say "Let's go do it" instead of "you."

6. **Sells instead of tells** - A servant leader is the opposite of a dictator. It's a style all about persuading, not commanding.

7. **It's not all about them** - There's a selfless quality about a servant leader. Someone who is thinking only, "How does this benefit me?" is disqualified.

8. **Thinks long-term** - A servant leader is thinking about the next generation, the next leader, and the next opportunity. That means a tradeoff between what's essential today versus tomorrow, and making choices to benefit the future.

9. **Acts with humility** - The leader doesn't wear a title as a way to show who's in charge, doesn't think he is better than everyone else, and acts in a way to care for others. They may pick up the trash or clean up a table. Setting an example of service, the servant leader understands that it is not about the leader, but about others.

Things to Avoid

Multitasking

People often boast about how good they are at multitasking. They think they are getting more done by juggling multiple tasks at once, but studies show that they aren't. When people multitask, their productivity decreases by as much as 40%.

Paying attention to multiple communication media at the same time, such as texting while listening to a colleague, may best be characterized as the "illusion of multitasking." Unlike listening to music and writing a report, which may be accomplished simultaneously, trying to communicate through multiple media channels usually does not result in positive outcomes.

Procrastination

Procrastination is the habit of delaying or putting off doing something that should be done right away. Everyone procrastinates sometimes. But when people procrastinate, they run the risk of jeopardizing their projects—and their reputations.

Micromanaging

While micromanaging may be necessary for some employees don't let this be your overall management styles. Micromanaging an employee or a team will only slow you down. There are just so many hours in each workweek, and your time working each week will start to creep up. Most employees despise "the micromanager," and it can damage your relationship with the employee and can come across as if you do not trust them.

Dismissing Other's Ideas

Dismissing other's ideas is generally a bad move, and you should never have your employees feel like you do not value their opinion.

3
Micromanagement

"The best executive is the one who has sense enough to pick good men to do what he wants done, and self-restraint enough to keep from meddling with them while they do it."

- Theodore Roosevelt

MICROMANAGING HAS ADVERSE EFFECTS on employees and causes a decrease in productivity. Micromanagement is not only a horrible leadership style as it has negative impacts on the organization, but it also has adverse effects on the employees that work for that organization. Understanding leadership styles is an essential step in identifying your strengths and weaknesses. Being a strong leader and avoiding micromanagement is not only crucial for the leader in the role, but it is also critical for the organization as a whole. Having strong leadership skills is essential for the employees that work for that organization.

First and foremost, micromanaging has a direct and negative impact on employee productivity. By not being a micromanager allows the employee to "fly on their own" and is found to be 21% more productive than someone who is not being micromanaged.

Micromanagement impacts the organization as studies have found that turnover is my higher for the company. Employee turnover can be 25% higher, which in the end effects the productivity of your employees. While in some cases, micromanagement may increase productivity over the short term, but long-term problems will eventually defeat any short-term gains.

Micromanaging employees has other negative impacts on employees such as, they no longer take risks, creativity dries up, and customer service goes down. The micromanager severely damages the productivity of the organization and, over the long run, may jeopardize the organization's survival.

Key Characteristics of the Micromanager

Watching Too Closely

Micromanagers tend to oversee their employees too closely and spend a lot of time supervising over a project or the daily operations. The micromanager needs to know specific details of their employee's schedule, plan, meetings, and other work-related conversations.

Difficulty Delegating

Micromanagers have a problem with trusting in their employees to complete a task themselves and will, in return, end up owning the responsibility. This is usually caused by a lack of trust between the parties.

Consistently Overextending

Micromanagers are consistently overextending themselves and their staff, and they will usually take on too many different projects. It is difficult for the micromanager to understand why they are so busy when tasks are itemized; they may not ever come to realize they are trying to do all of the jobs of the organization.

Must Be Right

The micromanager must be right at all costs, and they are always looking to place blame on everyone around them but themselves. They will be the first ones to throw their employees right under the bus. This creates a toxic environment and increases the stress levels of the employees, ultimately impacting morale.

If You Realize You're a Micromanager

You may now realize that you are a micromanager, and that is ok. The excellent news is recognizing and accepting that you are one is the first step to correcting it. It is not uncommon for micromanagers to change their management styles after learning; there are better ways to lead your team.

Let them Fail

For most individuals to learn and grow, it is essential to let them fail. Micromanagers usually hold not only themselves but others to strict standards as they are perfectionists. Let the employee falter and stammer to understand why they shouldn't perform the task in a certain way. After all, you have learned that along the way at some point, and some of the toughest lessons are the ones that are usually not forgotten.

Let Them Come to You

You will want to encourage an open line of communication. It is essential to set expectations when a task or project is assigned to have them come to you with any questions or concerns they may have. Sometimes it is best to wait for them to approach you if they have any questions or concerns.

Give More Responsibility

Give your employees more responsibility that you feel comfortable with providing them. While this may not be easy to do initially, but the more often you do, it will get easier.

Don't Dictate Everything

So now that you are giving out more responsibility, it is essential that you do not provide a specific roadmap on how to complete a project or task. Allow the employee some freedom to figure out how to achieve it on their own. As previously mentioned, set expectations, but you shouldn't spell it out for them.

Learn to Trust

Most micromanagers have trust issues, and they do so because of this. Remember that not everyone can perform the job precisely the way you want it. Take a more in-depth look at yourself and confront your issues with this.

Focus on Management

Perhaps you were the best operator before you moved into your leadership role, and your understanding of the material your employees handle is far superior. It is essential to understand that you are now a manager and leader of the group. You need to excel at your new role and focus on being that manager and leader. Let your team perform the tasks they need to, and you need to focus on management tasks.

Ways to Combat Being Micromanaged

Don't assume because you are now in a leadership position that you will not be micromanaged. It is not uncommon for managers themselves to be micromanaged by their supervisor. The good news is there are a few ways to combat being micromanaged.

Assess Your Own Behavior

Determine if there is a specific reason why your supervisor is micromanaging you. Sometimes those micromanaging us have a good reason, evaluate yourself, and see if there are certain areas that your supervisor continues to focus on or is continuously doing this.

Challenge Your Supervisor

Talk with your supervisor and address your concern with them, perhaps they can provide you some insight and set expectations on what they expect from you. There is nothing wrong talking about this and seeing if there is a common ground you both can reach.

Frequent Communication

Keeping your supervisor in the loop is a great way to combat being micromanagement. It builds trust between the two of you and shows that you are not trying to go rogue. It also demonstrates your competency when you are staying on tops of the tasks or projects assigned to you.

Anticipate Their Needs

Most micromanagers have triggers that and you can develop a sense of what those are. This will help you expect this type of behavior and will lower your stress. Once you have identified their triggers, it will allow you to stay one step ahead of them.

Things to Avoid

Owning Everything

It is important to not own every task or project. You must learn to rely on your staff and make sure you are delegating when needed. If this is a hard habit to break, setup a weekly or biweekly meeting to get brought up to speed on the progress.

Controlling Everything

Understand that you cannot control everything and that there is no way to predict every situation. Something will eventually go wrong and it is better to allow the employee who owns the task or project to attempt to fix it themselves.

Being Overbearing

It is important to step back and let your team members manage themselves. Do not check in on them hourly and set some guidelines for yourself. Employees hate nothing more than to have their boss hovering over them throughout the day.

Immerse Themselves

Micromanagers have the tendency to immerse themselves in overseeing the projects of others. They will reason that they not only need to be involved in this project but somehow is a reflection of themselves.

Discourage Others

Avoid discouraging others at all costs. It will make your team feel as though all decisions make must go through you. As a leader, if you value your own time and want to create a positive environment for your team to grow, you must encourage them.

4
Emotional Intelligence

"No one cares how much you know, until they know how much you care."

- *Theodore Roosevelt*

EMOTIONAL INTELLIGENCE is not a new concept. While the first published term 'Emotional Intelligence' was used in an article in 1990 by Peter Salovey and John D. Mayer, leaders have understood the importance of this concept throughout history.

For most people, emotional intelligence (EQ) is more important than intelligence (IQ) in attaining success in their lives and careers. As leaders, our success depends on our ability to read other people's signals and react appropriately to them.

When you think of a "perfect leader," what comes to mind? You might picture someone who never lets his temper get out of control, no matter what problems he's facing. Or you might think of someone who has the complete trust of her staff, listens to her team, is easy to talk to, and always makes careful, informed decisions. These are qualities of someone with a high degree of emotional intelligence.

34

To be effective, leaders must have a solid understanding of how their emotions and actions affect them. The better a leader relates to and works with others, the more successful he or she will be.

Practice Self Awareness

Being self-aware means that you have a sharp realization of your personality, including your strengths and weaknesses, your thoughts and beliefs, your emotions, and your motivations. The ability to be self-aware is one of the most essential yet challenging skills we as leaders can achieve.

1. Break Visceral Reactions

A person without self-awareness runs on auto-pilot and responds with knee-jerk reactions. Self-awareness allows you to assess situations objectively and rationally, without acting on biases and stereotypes.

Take a deep breath before you act, especially when a situation triggers anger or frustration. This gives you time to re-assess whether your response will be the best one.

2. The Three Why's

The three why's technique was developed by Sakichi Toyoda and used by Toyota to evolve its manufacturing approach. It explores the cause-and-effect relationships underlying a particular problem. By repeating the question "Why?" you dig deeper into the root cause.

Before acting on a decision, ask yourself, "Why?" Follow up your response with another "Why?" And then a third. If you can find three good reasons to pursue something, you'll have clarity and confidence in your actions.

3. Improve Your Body Language Awareness

Watching yourself on video can be a cringeworthy experience, but awareness of your body language, posture, and mannerisms improves your confidence.

Slouching, or taking a "low-power-pose" increases cortisol and feeds low self-esteem while standing tall or taking a "high-power-pose" stimulates testosterone and improves your performance. Using hand gestures helps with articulating your thoughts and affects how people respond to you.

Learn To Motivate Yourself

Motivation can give you that extra push to get something done, but it doesn't always come when you need it. We have trouble keeping the fire lit from time to time. It's so much easier to sit back and think about all the things we're going to do eventually.

Some days you feel it, and other days you can't grab a measly corner of it no matter how hard you try, so it is essential to set yourself up for success.

1. Avoid Distractions

Turn off your phone, find a quiet place, make sure that your workspace is tidy and comfortable to keep you free from distractions. There is nothing worse than starting something just to be distracted, which can kill your motivation.

2. Break Things Down

If you feel the task at hand is too big, it can feel like you aren't making any progress. Try breaking a big job down into manageable sections with a clear starting point. For example, you could start off brainstorming then plot the next stages. By making the work more manageable, you should find that your motivation returns.

3. Work With Others

Have you ever heard the saying, "iron sharpens iron?" This applies to motivation, and sometimes it is helpful to work directly with someone. You need to be mindful of who you choose and make sure they are equally motivated and positive.

4. Stay Positive

When it comes to motivation, you can be your own worst critic. To push yourself to do what you need to, give yourself positive affirmations. Remember that you can get this task done if you put your mind to it. Tell yourself that you can accomplish anything.

5. Give Yourself A Break

While it is essential to avoid distractions, too much work can make you less productive. Schedule occasional breaks throughout your day. Make sure you also take longer breaks over the weekend to rest and refresh yourself. Give yourself occasional breaks to avoid burnout.

Know Your Stressors

Effective stress management starts with identifying your sources of stress and developing strategies to manage them. Stress is your body's reaction to the demands of the world. Stressors are events or conditions in your surroundings that may trigger anxiety. Your body responds to stressors differently depending on whether the stressor is new or short term acute stress or whether the stressor has been around for a longer time chronic stress.

Recognizing a problem is the first step toward solving it. By beginning to identify and understand the sources of your stress, you've taken the first step in learning to manage it better. Manage it, not eliminate it.

1. Track Your Stressors

This first step to identifying any problem is to recognize it. Keep a journal for a week or two to determine which situations create the most stress and how you respond to them. Record your thoughts, feelings, and information about the environment, including the people and circumstances involved, the physical setting, and how you reacted.

2. Develop Healthy Responses

Instead of attempting to fight stress with fast food or alcohol, do your best to make healthy choices when you feel the tension rise. Exercise is a great stress-buster; any form of physical activity is beneficial.

Make time for hobbies and favorite activities. Whether it's reading a novel, going to concerts, or playing games with your family, make sure to set aside time for the things that please you. Getting enough good-quality sleep is also crucial for effective stress management.

3. Keep Your Perfectionism in Check

Being a high achiever can help you feel good about yourself and excel at work. Being a perfectionist, on the other hand, can drive you and the people around you little nuts. Especially in busy, fast-paced jobs, you may not be able to do everything correctly.

4. Prioritize Your Priorities

With competing deadlines and fast-changing priorities, it's critical to define what's truly important and why. It's essential to understand your role in the organization, its strategic priorities, and your personal goals and strengths. Take a look at your to-do list and focus on the projects that will have the most impact and are best aligned with your goals.

Be Mindful of Your Vocabulary

The workplace is one of the most challenging places to elicit a mindful state of being, as it is an environment that is often connected to stress and high-pressure tasks.

Language and words almost always critically translate into thoughts and feelings, thoughts and feelings which seem so intricately and intimately connected to who we are, to our sense of self. But we choose the words we use and can adjust our relationships to our own words, thoughts, and feelings.

What you say will have an impact not only on whom you speak them to, but also on you. Your words reflect your thoughts and feelings, so becoming mindful of them will help you to use them more wisely.

1. Develop a Higher Level of Presence

Presence is your ability to experience any moment, without thinking about the past or the future. When you are more present, you'll be more conscious of the words you use.

2. Develop Your Vocabulary

Most people stop learning when they finish their formal education, which means they don't improve their vocabulary. You can adjust your vocabulary through reading and learning a new word a day.

3. Pause and Listen

If a conversation takes a negative tone and you'd instead not take part, it is a great time to take a step back and pause. There is no need to be additive. It's common to want to be seen and have our voice heard, but it's also refreshing to say less and listen more. When we practice listening, it becomes much easier to be thoughtful, kind, and intentional with the words we use.

Recognize Emotions in Others

There are several ways that we can tell how others are feeling, but mainly by observing what they say and how they behave. Research suggests that more than 80% of communication is non-verbal, meaning that it comes from body language and facial expression.

1. Use your Ears

If you want to know how someone is feeling, it might be better to close your eyes and use your ears: People tend to read others' emotions more accurately when they listen and don't look.

2. Read Their Faces

Human beings around the world have similar brain structures and use similar facial muscles to express basic emotions such as happiness, sadness, fear, surprise, anger, and disgust. The face is the best indicator of a person's feelings. Yet, it often is overlooked.

3. Read Their Body Language

Body language provides a fantastic amount of information on what other people are thinking if you know what to look for. An example of this is crossed arms and legs are physical barriers that suggest the other person is not open to what you're saying—crossed legs or arms signal that a person is mentally, emotionally, and physically blocked from what's in front of them.

You can't read a person's exact thoughts, you can learn a lot from their body language, which is especially true when words and body language don't match.

Things to Avoid

Emotional Repression

Emotionally intelligent people don't push away their feelings, even the unpleasant ones. They're in tune with everything from joy to fury, anxiety, and ambivalence, and they let themselves genuinely experience the whole gamut of emotions.

Unnecessary Conflict

While it's good to stand up for yourself and be direct in communication, it's emotionally smart to avoid becoming embroiled in fights that go nowhere. Pick and choose your battles according to what truly matters. Don't waste your energy on bickering or jealous competitions, and save that power for positive interactions instead.

Gossip

Gossiping is another type of negative interaction that's best avoided. It's pointless at best and harmful at worst. Plus, it marks you out as the sort of person who can't be trusted. Emotionally intelligent people strive for more in-depth, more meaningful conversations rather than focusing on rumors. They're mindful of the fact that words can wound.

Don't Dismiss Other's Feelings

Empathy is another significant characteristic of highly emotionally intelligent people. It means that you deeply understand how someone else feels, and try to put yourself in their shoes. People with a high EQ don't disregard how others feel; on the contrary, they want to decode others' feelings because they have such compassion for them. They can anticipate other people's needs and are highly perceptive.

Saying Yes Too Often

Emotionally strong leaders realize that people have limits, including them, and they can't possibly say yes to everyone. So they know their boundaries. Furthermore, they honor themselves by sticking to their guns and only agreeing to activities and tasks that they can reasonably accomplish.

Don't Seek Approval From Others

If they want something, they go after it without feeling the need to consult others. They validate themselves, so they don't require others to do it for them. While they respectfully listen to other people's opinions, they don't let other's views form the basis for their decisions in life. They know that as long as they approve of themselves, they can achieve whatever they desire.

Avoid Dwelling on Problems

When you fixate on the problems that you're facing, you create and prolong negative emotions and stress, which hinders performance. When you focus on actions to better yourself and your circumstances, you create a sense of personal efficacy that produces positive emotions and improves performance. Emotionally intelligent people won't dwell on problems because they know they're most effective when focusing on solutions.

SECTION TWO

BEST PRACTICES

Best Practices (Plural Noun) best prac-tices - A procedure that has been shown by research and experience to produce optimal results and that is established or proposed as a standard suitable for widespread adoption

Synonyms: application, exercise, use, operation, implementation, execution;

5
Communication

"I speak to everyone the same way, whether he is the garbage man or the president of the university."

- *Albert Einstein*

DON'T ONLY BE A GREAT SPEAKER, be a great communicator. There are few things more important than communication. As a leader, you must make sure you are consistently focused on your communication skill sets as it can be challenging for most leaders. The information you send and receive are not only crucial during a typical day but even more critical during challenging days.

The fact that effective communication is a crucial ingredient for success is rather apparent to most people. However, poor communication is one of the most common issues that exist within an organization. Some barriers that contribute to this is perceptual and attributional biases, interpersonal relationships, top management's role, gender differences, physical distance, and organization structure can create cause communication breakdown.

We live in a world where communication has improved dramatically within the past few decades, thanks to the advancement of technology. It is not hard to get overwhelmed with all the ways anyone can reach you to you at any given time. It is essential to keep in mind that mismanaging the way people communicate with you, and vice-versa can be a drain on your efficiencies. There a quite few things you can do to keep from getting stressed out and remain an effective leader and be the "great communicator."

In business, poor communication costs money and wastes time. One study found that 14% of each workweek is wasted on poor communication. In contrast, effective communication is an asset for organizations and individuals alike. Effective communication skills, for example, are an asset for job seekers.

Types of Communication

Communication can be categorized into three basic types, including (1) verbal communication, in which you listen to a person to understand the meaning; (2) written communication, in which you read meaning; (3) nonverbal communication, in which you observe a person and infer meaning. Each of these types has its advantages and disadvantages.

Email

Thomas Jefferson summed up the rules of writing well with this idea: "Don't use two words when one will do." Put another way; half the words can have twice the impact. One of the oldest myths in business is that writing more will make you sound more important, but the opposite is true. Leaders who can communicate simply and clearly project a stronger image than those who write a lot but say nothing.

Stay Current

If staying on top of your email is an issue for you, it is best to put some time on your calendar if needed for administrative work. Email must be read every workday, and it is easy to fall behind or even get in the habit of not checking daily. Like it or not, email is just a part of the job, and it is essential to stay on top of it.

Set an Out of Office

Make sure you have an "Out of Office Message" when you are not in the office. Make sure that the out of office message include the day(s) you are out and also when you are expected to return. Offer an alternative or backup they can contact if possible.

Read Twice, Send Once

Before sending out an email, it is crucial that you review it at least twice. This will not only help you make sure you are sending out the right message, but it will also prevent you from looking foolish.

When Sending Out Mass Emails

When sending out an email to large groups of people, it is best to include all employees in the BCC field. By using the BCC field, it will prevent employees from sending replies to everyone on the email. This will reduce the amount of email clutter, and everyone on the email will appreciate this.
Be detailed when sending out mass emails — ensuring that all the important dates, contacts, places, and pertinent information will reduce the number of further questions or concerns people may have.

Desk Phone

Set up your voicemail

This may seem like an obvious one, but I have encountered this one countless times. You can come across as unorganized or as if you don't care if you do not have your voicemail setup.

Professional Voicemail Greeting

Make sure that your voicemail greeting is professional. It is vital to make sure your voicemail message uses the appropriate tone, word usage, and that the voicemail message is not too long.

Call Back

Return all calls within a timely fashion; when you receive a voicemail, don't procrastinate. If you received a lot of calls prioritize who gets called back first.

Again, Set an Out of Office

Make sure you have an "Out of Office message" on both your desk phone and or cell phone. It is not the responsibility of the caller to know your schedule.

Make sure that the out of office message include the day(s) you are out and also when you are expected to return. Offer an alternate contact or backup contact that they can call if possible.

Cell Phone

Text Messages

Text messages are becoming increasingly more popular as a form of communication for job requests. If possible, I would avoid using this as a primary mode of communication. There are times that we need to tune out the phone calls and texts.

While it may be hard to disconnect, sometimes there are times that it is necessary. The other concern is a text could be personal or business, and staying focused on work can be difficult if you are receiving a lot of personal text messages.

Set an Out of Office!

I know I sound like a broken record, however, if people are reaching out to you on your cell phone for business, make sure you are also putting an out of office message on your phone when you are on vacation, sick, or holiday.

Instant Messaging

Use Sparingly

More and more companies are using instant messaging as a form of communicating. While this is a great way to get answers to quick questions, keep in mind that it can rob someone's focus. It essential that you are using this sparingly.

Communicate Back

If you do not have time to speak with someone at that time, let them know and get back with them when you have more time. Turn this off or set it to "do not disturb" when you need to concentrate. Someone could potentially reach out to you at any time and break that concentration.

Group Messaging

Use Only For Urgent Messages

Sometimes emailing urgent messages can be too slow and can be missed by some. Using group messaging can be a great tool to use when communicating urgent messages that need to be sent out.

You can create a group for your team as well as for leadership communications. This will help organize mass communications, which can be catered to your audience.

It is also essential to make sure that you are setting the rules. This type of communication should be used for urgent issues, only not to talk about trivial topics or topics that can wait to be discussed face to face.

Don't Have One on One Conversations

Group messages are meant to disseminate information and work collaboratively with your teams—any message that requires multiple groups or individuals; it is excellent to use this space.

This space, however, should not be used to for one on one conversations with your peers. Team messaging can be extremely disruptive, especially when individuals are in meetings. If you want to have a conversation with someone directly, pick up the phone or message them individually. Your group will thank you.

One on One Employee Sessions

Perform Monthly 1:1's

Performing one on ones are a great way to get to better under connect with your employees. Make sure you are completing your one on ones with all of your employees each month.

If you have more than 25 employees, perform these quarterly. Otherwise, you find that this is taking up a lot of your time that could probably be focused elsewhere.

Give Them Time

While it is essential to cover the requested questions set forth by your leadership, it is necessary to allow the employee time to speak about whatever is on their mind. As a leader, it is good practice to hold your thoughts and will enable the employee to do most of the talking. Do 80% of the listening and 20% of the talking.

Public Speaking

Public speaking is difficult for most people. There are an estimated 87% of all Americans have glossophobia, which is a fear of public speaking. So you are not alone, and most audience speakers understand this and understand the difficulties of public speaking.

Be prepared!

How do you get to Carnegie Hall? Practice, Practice, Practice. If you have a presentation that you need to present, give yourself some time with it, bring it home and practice it behind closed doors. By having dry runs of your presentation, this will allow you to be more comfortable with the content.

Know your Audience

Remember who you are speaking to and tailor the message for them. Try to leave the jargon out of the presentation unless the audience is knowledgeable on the material. If you look out to the crowd and see their eyes glazed over, it is time to re-evaluate your approach.

Be Yourself

Don't try to be anyone else but yourself when speaking in front of an audience. You may not come across as genuine and lose some of the audience.

Tell A Story

Being able to connect to your audience is crucial. Adding a personal touch to your presentation can affect the material you are presenting as it draws your audience into your presentation.

Keep Your Energy Level High

There is nothing worse than a speaker that has low energy. They can suck the energy right out of the room, and instead of engaging their audience, they find themselves disconnecting from them.

Paperwork

While physical paperwork becomes less common due to the advancement of technology and communications, there is still plenty of it in the work environment.

Don't Keep Everything

Avoid the clutter, if a paper communication doesn't require a response from you, skim it, and then toss or file it. If a paper communication requests a response from you, respond immediately, then throw it away, file it, or shred it.

Stay Organized

Stay organized with the paperwork and keep it in specific folders if you need to retain a physical copy. If you're too busy to respond right away, put the document in a "Later" file. Be sure to rank the items by priority.

Scan What You Can

If you don't need to keep a physical copy of the paperwork then scan it on a copier and keep in organized on your computer.

Shred What You Don't Need

Shred any work documents that you don't need; this will ensure the communication will remain confidential and help out the environment.

Stay up to Date

Go through your documents every so often, say once a quarter to see if the information is still relevant. If you are not sure if you still need it, scan it!

Listen Deeply

While we may have covered outward communication, it is equally important to listen deeply to others. By knowing your constituents, listening to them, and taking their advice, leaders give voice to their constituents' feelings.

The best leaders are great listeners. They listen carefully to what other people have to say and how they feel. They ask good (and often tough) questions, are open to ideas other than their own, and even lose arguments in support of the common good. Through intense listening, leaders get a sense of what people want, what they value, and what they dream about.

Extraordinary things can happen when leaders listen—when they involve employees in identifying issues, hear their frustrations and their aspirations, and find ways to respond with initiatives that address those concerns. Generating excitement in a workplace is possible when leaders pay attention to what people want and need.

Things to Avoid

Avoid To Many Audiovisuals

When speaking publicly and presenting, it is vital to keep the audiovisuals, such as videos, to a minimum. Having too many breaks during your presentation can cause a disconnect between you are your audience.

Stay Focused

When having conversations with people, avoid multitasking. You must be present for the discussion regardless of how menial it may seem.

Pick Up the Phone

When you need a direct answer or something that requires a high level of detail, pick up the phone. Sometimes it is just easier, and quicker to pick up the phone and talk about it.

Just Digital

Impersonal "digital" communication is relatively fast and easier to do than more personal communication forms, senders are often not as practiced or as skilled in the more personal modes.

Electronic communication systems are invaluable to today's organizations, but they have considerable limitations when it comes to bringing about change. Don't just use digital modes of communication, understand that is equally important to have some facetime in with your peers and stakeholders.

Leave Emotion out of Emails

Emails are great when you need to send out a communication with facts. It can be difficult to convey emotion in emails, and when attempted, it could easily be misconstrued. If you need to send a message with feeling, it is best to do this verbally.

Don't Email Everything

Sometimes face to face conversations makes more sense when the sender is conveying a sensitive or emotional message. If the sender needs feedback immediately and does not require a permanent record of the conversation have a face to face conversation with the individual.

6
Time Management

"Don't be fooled by the calendar. There are only as many days in the year as you make use of. One man gets only a week's value out of a year while another man gets a full year's value out of a week."

- *Charles Dow Richards*

TIME MANAGEMENT IS VITAL as your calendar is going to start getting filled up. Email. Voicemail. Meetings. Paperwork. Employee Engagement. Projects. Essential requests from multiple people at once. Direct reports who continually ask for help or bring you their problems. There is no question that it is crucial to have strong time management skills.

Time management is all about remaining organized. The more organized you are, the better you can effectively manage time for projects, requests, and your employees. If you can control time better, this can lower your stress levels.

Managing Your Time Effectively

Time management is more than just deciding you'll spend 30 minutes on one task and an hour on another. It is also about organizing your tasks to see what needs to be accomplished through your day and setting priorities.

Manage Your Time Effectively

Clarify Your Goals

First, you need to identify your priorities, so you can use your time in the best way possible to accomplish them. Without setting priorities, you run the risk of putting off important tasks and not meeting deadlines.

Assess How You Use Your Time

It is crucial to track your time and look for ways to improve how you spend it. You should only need to do this occasionally if you find you, there is never enough time in the day to accomplish all of your tasks.

By tracking your time over a week, you can start to identify where your time is being spent and adjust as needed.

Devise a Plan

If you are not already, it is essential to start creating schedules and to-do lists that map out how you plan to spend your time. This will help you streamline your time management.

Implement Your Plan

Now that you have identified how you are spending your time and have created your to-do lists and schedules, you need to hold yourself accountable. By putting your strategy in place and executing your plan, it will protect yourself from distractions that can prevent you from executing that plan.

Improve Your Plan

Just like any good plan it is important to understand they are fluid and can change. You need to assess your progress toward achieving your goals and adjust your approach as needed.

Examples of Time Management

"Time Blocking"

Time Blocking is a method that is used by blocking time on your calendar to specific tasks it helps hold yourself accountable. An example of this would be to set time aside to perform admin tasks like email.

If you start finding some tasks more difficult to accomplish, then set time aside for that task and close your door over or put some headsets on.

Have a Task List

Capture the tasks and activities you must do on a list and update it regularly during the day. Revisit this list frequently and add new items as soon as they appear. Make sure your list gives you a quick overview of everything urgent and important, and remember to include strategic and relationship-building activities as well as operational tasks.

Minimize Interruptions

The more uninterrupted time you get during the day to work on essential tasks, the more effective you will be. Identify the activities that tend to disrupt your work, and find a solution. For example, avoid checking emails and answering the phone when you're in the middle of something important.

Delegate

If you are to add maximum value to your day, you must learn to delegate. By adequately delegating and empowering your employees, it can help you create time to concentrate on the big picture and the strategic aspects of your top agendas of the day.

Be Organized

Being organized might sound like an obvious recommendation; however, being organized can be a constant struggle for some new and seasoned leaders. The more organized you are, the better your stress levels will be, and you'll have more control over time management.

Identify Your Time Management Style

Think about your time management style by reflecting on some key areas. It is essential to understand your time management style and determine where you need to improve.

First, you will need to identify what your motivation is for managing your time. For an example, perhaps you find you are spending too much time at your desk, or are just working too many hours during the week, you need to find out what your motivation is to improve your time management.

You will also need to identify what your current time management abilities are. By identifying your strengths and weaknesses, you can start to build your base.

Your biggest time management challenges need to be identified as well. It is vital to determine your problems to overcome them. Specific tasks can that give you energy—and those that can sap it. While some tasks are unavoidable, perhaps you need to look at your approach to them and change how you handle them.

We are all different, and there are some times of day when you're most and least focused. For some, it is early in the day while others it is midday. Once you identify what time of the day you have the most energy, start to pile on the tasks during those times.

Family Comes First!

We put all this emphasis on time-management at work and being able to perform your job efficiently, remember however that family always comes first and if you need to reschedule something for your family (emergency, important family event, etc.) Reschedule!

Things to Avoid

Delegating To The Wrong Person

Delegating work will save you hours if you are empowering to the right people. Appointing a job to the wrong person could end up increasing the workload if it is not done correctly. Ensure you are delegating to an individual with the right skillsets.

Don't Take On Too Much

Don't take on too much responsibility. If you are asked to take on additional work and say yes to everyone, then you run the risk of taking on too much. While it may be hard, but sometimes, you have to say "no."

Keep A To-Do List

Failing to keep a to-do list is a significant time management mistake. With all of the tasks you have to do daily, it can be challenging to keep it straight. The last thing you need is to remember something you forgot to do on your way home. It can ruin your night.

Today, Not Tomorrow

Don't procrastinate, do what you can today and not tomorrow. The more you delay, the more work piles up and increases your stress levels. Sometimes all you need to do is to stay late and wrap up your tasks for the day.

7
Meetings

"The number of meetings I've been in – people would be shocked. But that's how you gain experience, how you can gain knowledge, being in meetings and participating. You learn and grow."

- *Tiger Woods*

OH, THE DREADED MEETINGS! Some days/weeks can be filled with them. The more you move up that corporate ladder, you will inevitably have more and more meetings. If you are not hosting the meeting, it is essential that you are engaged. Whether it is a meeting that is on the phone, a WebEx, or at a physical location, you must remain engaged at all times.

When I first made my transition into a management role, I was surprised by the number of meetings that I needed to attend: the weekly project meetings, monthly team meetings the quarterly updates, biannual updates, and annual updates.

Anyone who has been part of a team knows that it involves team meetings. While few individuals relish the idea of meetings, they serve an essential function in terms of information sharing and decision making. They are also an important social function that can help build team cohesion and coordinate task functions.

Teleconference or Web Conferencing

Make sure you are always announcing yourself when speaking in large groups on a teleconference. Not everyone knows your voice, and it can get very confusing for all parties when you do not announce yourself.

It is important to remember to put yourself on mute. This will avoid any background noise that the rest of the audience can hear. Also, it can prevent any awkward conversations you may be having while you are waiting for the meeting to being.

Arrive early if possible; this will allow you to prepare for the meeting if needed.

When Hosting a Meeting

Before the Meeting

Decide who should be at the meeting and only invite those people. The more people who attend a meeting, the less each person will participate, so there should be a reason why each person is invited to the meeting. Consider who should be there and limit your invitation to those individuals.

Have an agenda! By having a plan, it will help keep the meeting stay on the topic. A plan will inform those invited about the purpose of the meeting. It also helps organize the flow of the meeting and keep the team on track.

Send a reminder before the meeting, reminding everyone of the purpose, time, and location of a meeting helps everyone prepare themselves. If a team meets only to find that there is no reason for the meeting because members haven't completed their agreed-upon tasks, team performance or morale can be negatively impacted.

During and After the Meeting

Make sure that someone is taking meeting minutes and writing down essential keynotes, such as dates, names, projects, etc. If no one can be assigned, then the host should do their best to take critical notes and send them out to those that have attended after the meeting is over.

If you are the host, it is essential to start on time and to be mindful of other people's time. Waiting for members who are running late only punishes those who are on time and reinforces the idea that it's okay to be late.

Announce who the key stakeholders on the call. There is no need to go into great detail, just their name, and their title is usually enough.

When the meeting veers off-topic as the host, it is essential to set the meeting back in the right direction. Veering off from the agenda communicates to members that the agenda is not crucial. It also makes it difficult for others to keep track of where you are in the meeting.

Summarize the meeting with action items. Be sure to clarify team member roles moving forward. If individuals' tasks are not precise, the chances are that role confusion will arise later. There should be clear notes from the meeting regarding who is responsible for each action item and the time frames associated with the next steps.

Make sure that you are ending the meeting on time. Concluding the meeting on time is vitally important, as it shows that you respect everyone's time and are organized. If another meeting is needed to follow up, schedule it later, but don't let the meeting run over.

Things to Avoid

Is the Meeting Needed?

Leaders should do a number of things prior to a meeting to make it more effective, the first being to make sure the meeting is even needed. If the meeting is primarily informational in nature, ask yourself if it is imperative that the group fully understands the information and if future decisions will be built upon this information. If so, a meeting may be needed. If not, perhaps simply communicating with everyone in a written format will save valuable time.

Give the Pen a Break

It is great that you are taking notes however taking too many notes can leave you unengaged in the meeting. Find a balance between taking notes when needed and staying engaged in the meeting.

Don't get distracted... Focus!

It is crucial to remain focused and engaged in the meeting. These days there are so many devices that can rob us of our focus, like our phone or computer.

Try to leave your computer behind; It is common for leaders to discourage flat out bringing a laptop to a meeting.

Turn your phone off or over. If possible disconnect from your phone as well. This is just another tool to rob you from your focus.

Back to Back Meetings

It is good to have at least 10-15 mins in between meeting to reflect on the meeting that was just had and collect your thoughts. So it is important to avoid scheduling back to back meetings if you can.

While avoiding meetings back to back is not always possible if anything else, be mindful to limit this is possible.

If you are setting a meeting and forego the last 10 minutes of the meeting set up the meeting for 50-minute intervals instead of the hour. Everyone at the meeting with a busy schedule will appreciate it.

Watch out for Double Booking

If this is unavoidable make sure you set up a proxy in your place in one of the meetings and try to get your proxy up to speed as best you can.

Not Being Prepared

Not being prepared is just not acceptable, if you are invited to a meeting and expectations are set, do not go to the meeting unprepared.

Mute your Cell Phone

If you cannot turn your cell phone off mute it. If you must take a call and are in a physical meeting then leave the meeting that you are in and taking the phone call is proper etiquette. It is bad form to take the call in the room when a meeting is going on.

Don't Announce Yourself When arriving Late

There is no need to announce yourself when you are late for a meeting; it will most likely interrupt the speaker and throw off the pace of the meeting. Frankly speaking, it is just rude and inconsiderate to announce yourself when you are late.

SECTION THREE

Employee Interaction

Employee (Noun) em-ploy-ee - A person employed for wages or salary, especially at nonexecutive level.

Synonyms: worker, working man/woman, member of staff, staffer, blue-collar worker, white-collar worker, laborer, workingman, hand, hired hand, wage earner; personnel, staff, workforce;

8
Hiring/Interviewing

"You need to have a collaborative hiring process."

- *Steve Jobs*

HIRING AND INTERVIEWING is another crucial skillset that you must continuously improve. Having the right fit for your team is extremely important, and having someone toxic could spread like cancer to the rest of the group. I cannot emphasize the importance of spending time on the hiring process.

It is essential to put some focus on becoming a good interviewer. Ensuring that you are an excellent interviewer almost guarantees that when you interview someone, the experience is comfortable for both you and the interviewee.

Hiring/Interviewing

Hiring Panel

Practice

The more interviewing opportunities, the better, try to get involved in as many interviews as possible. It is not uncommon to sit on the hiring panel for other departments, so if you see an opportunity, grab it.

Use the Same Questions

Be consistent with questioning when interviewing multiple candidates. This will ensure how each candidate responds to the same questions.

Identify the Questions

There are great interview questions and other recommendations when performing an interview. It is essential to do some research to find some the right interview questions that would be helpful to practice.

Use an Interview Grid

When interviewing multiple potential employees, it is good to use an interview grid. An interview grid allows you to rate the interviewee during the interview process. This is helpful only to identify or "grade" the employee's strengths and weaknesses. It could be used whether you are on a panel or interviewing one on one.

Know the Candidates

It is important to make sure you thoroughly go through the candidates resumes prior to interviewing them. Resumes are a great way to look at their background information and give you an opportunity to cross exam them based on the information that they have provided.

Nonverbal Communication

Research shows that nonverbal cues can also affect whether you get a candidate gets a job. Judges examining videotapes of actual applicants were able to assess the social skills of job candidates with the sound turned off.

They watched the rate of gesturing, time spent talking, and the formality of dress to determine which candidates would be the most successful socially on the job. For this reason, it is essential to consider how we appear in business as well as what we say. The muscles of our faces convey our emotions, so we can send a silent message without saying a word.

Ask Behavioral Based Questions

Depending on the job you are interviewing for this may or may not seem obvious. For example, if this is for a Human Resource position, it only makes sense to ask behavioral questions. However, if this is for a technical job, it may be more difficult to understand why this is needed.

Asking questions for problem-solving skills or integrity questions can provide insight on the potential employee that you may have otherwise looked over during the interview process and peel the surface back a bit to see if they may or may not get along with your team.

- Behavioral Based Question Example #1 - **Problem Solving:** Tell me about an experience in which you turned a problem into a success.

- Behavioral Based Question Example #2 – **Integrity:** When was the last time you 'broke the rules?' What was the situation and what did you do?

Setup Back to Back Interviews

This will help with consistency and tone when asking questions. It will also help with the flow of the meeting. Identify who will start with the questions and the order of who will go next.

Peer Panels

This is a great way to get feedback from your team for a potential hire. It also makes them feel like they are more involved in the process.

Ensure that the employees that you are going to perform the interview are adequately trained or coached. This can be uncomfortable for all parties if they are not trained on interview questions.

Onboarding

Not having a smooth onboarding is a major complaint from most new employees and can be a painful experience for most new employees. Onboarding is a crucial area needed to be focused on for any new employees. So it is essential for you to have a plan!

Many organizations, take a more structured and systematic approach to new employee onboarding, while others follow a "sink or swim" approach in which new employees struggle to figure out what is expected of them and what the norms are.

Have a Program

An orientation program is important, because it has a role in making new employees feel welcome in addition to imparting information that may help them to be successful in their new jobs.

Many large organizations have formal orientation programs consisting of lectures, videotapes, and written material, while some may follow more unusual approaches.

Formal orientation programs are helpful in teaching employees about the goals and history of the company, as well as communicating the power structure. Moreover, these programs may also help with a new employee's integration into the team.

Announcement

You've just hired this talented person for your team -- don't keep it quiet! Spread the word around, send out an email, get the word out! This will not only ensure that everyone is expecting a new co-worker, it will promote a positive and transparent environment.

Before Day 1

Keep in regular contact with your new hire. Send any paperwork that can be completed in advance so as not to slow down that first day.

Jargon Busting

I've yet to find a company that doesn't have its language and jargon. Whether it's those pesky acronyms that people use (but can't always explain!)

Rules of Engagement

Whether this is the new hire's first job or he or she has worked in the industry a long time, you *must* spend time explaining the rules of engagement, otherwise known as the corporate and team etiquette that ensures success.

Sweat the Small Stuff

Don't underestimate the impact of not addressing the small stuff. Which number is needed to dial an outside line? How do you use the photocopier? Where are the restrooms? Where is the coffee machine? When are lunch breaks taken? It's the little things that can be the most frustrating when we are new to a team and are trying to be at our best.

Provide A Mentor

Mentors can be crucial to helping new employees adjust by teaching them the ins and outs of their jobs and how the company really operates. A mentor is a trusted person who provides an employee with advice and support regarding career-related matters. Although a mentor can be any employee or manager who has insights that are valuable to the new employee, mentors tend to be relatively more experienced than their protégés.

Things to Avoid

Warm Bodies

Do not hire a "warm body." Sometimes it can be difficult to fill a spot, do not hire someone to fill the spot. Make sure they are the right fit for the job and find someone that will work well with the team.

Avoid Large Hiring Panels

Don't have huge panels of six or more people; this can be very intimidating to even the most skilled interviewee. Break down into smaller groups if possible

Marathon Interviews

Avoid the marathon interviews; Interviews do not need to exceed more than 60 minutes per session. Focus on the areas you would like to cover and if you find yourself continually going over 60 minutes to evaluate the questions and "trim the fat."

9
Evaluating Team Members

"Only the guy who isn't rowing has time to rock the boat."

- **Jean-Paul Sartre**

EVALUATING TEAM MEMBERS is an area that can often be overlooked or is an area where not enough emphasis is put on it. It is crucial that you feel comfortable evaluating your team. You need to make sure that they are meeting expectations and that they are held accountable.

It is crucial that as a leader, you are identifying strengths and weaknesses in the group. By Identifying strength and weaknesses, it will not only help you start to focus on specific individuals or teams to improve their weaknesses, but it will also help you leverage their strengths.

Most employees also want to receive feedback to ensure that they are doing a good job as well as help them grow and improve. Engaged employees care about their work and their company, and that begins with proper evaluation and giving appropriate feedback. By working closely and communicating with your team members, it also ensures that you have a good pulse and remain in tune with their needs and concerns.

Employee engagement and motivation varies depending on the individual. It is essential to identify why some employees choose to count the hours while others pursue excellence. Job performance is the result of three factors, which are, motivation, ability, and the environment.

Motivation is defined as the desire to achieve a goal or a certain performance level, leading to goal-directed behavior. Ability—or having the skills and knowledge required to perform the job—is also important and is sometimes the key determinant of effectiveness. Finally, environmental factors such as having the resources, information, and support one needs to perform well are critical to determining performance.

Why Care About Employee Engagement?

Some of the Benefits of Engaged Employees:

- Engaged employees perform 20% better than non-committed employees. You will find that a team that is engaged is more productive.

- Engaged employees are 87% more likely to stay with the organization. Company loyalty will also help with new hires as the culture is a positive one which is ultimately spread your employees.

- While it is important that all employees take some time off for themselves, engaged employees have 44% lower rates of absenteeism.
- No one likes working with someone that has a bad attitude. Engaged employees have on average 5% higher customer satisfaction rating than those that are not engaged.

- Organizations have found that engaged employees are also 10% higher profitability.

Engaged Employees Lead to:

- Overall increased work performance for both individuals and for teams.

- Increased employee retention, as engaged employees are less likely to leave the organization.

- Improved business outcomes, which meet the expectations of the leadership of the organization but also their customers.

Performing Monthly One on One's

Performing one on ones are crucial to getting a deeper understanding of the individual and help you build trust between the two of you. Performing 1:1's can be a great way to sit down and get to know your employees. This shouldn't be treated as a 15-minute conversation, and you should take this seriously and make it meaningful.

Do not treat as just something that you need to check off on your ever-growing list of things to do. This is one of the more crucial times that you will spend with your employees.

Evaluating Performance and Potential

- Be objective, specific, and reward accomplishment. Identify areas of needed growth or at least how they can make a good performance great.

- Do your best to provide information from first-hand knowledge.

- Engage high performers in conversation regarding their performance

- Align rewards and recognition to goal achievement and organizational priorities. For example; don't punish good performers by giving them more work. Don't reward poor performers by removing work.

Providing Feedback

When to Provide Feedback

It is important to identify when good work is performed. It is good habit as a leader to provide positive feedback.

When a problem is affecting important outcomes, you must set expectations and then provide feedback on the work. This will ensure the work being performed stays on the defined track.

How to Provide Feedback

Feedback can be formal, like a performance review or informal like a watercooler conversation. This will depend on the type of feedback, how crucial the feedback is, and the timeliness of said feedback. Informal feedback is usually ongoing, in the moment advice outside of formal performance reviews.

When providing feedback, you need to make sure that you are specific, relevant/balanced, and prompt. The employee must understand how critical the feedback is.

Feedback should be proactive and constructive. The employee should not feel like the feedback is an attack on their work.

Providing Positive Feedback

Be specific about the action that was taken and on the work that was performed. Discuss the impacts with the employee on the department, team, goals, etc. Make sure to tie the feedback to the mission and values whenever possible.

Be prompt about giving positive feedback. Do not wait too long when discussing feedback with the employee or team. Thank and recognize the team and or individuals for their excellent work. This can be done one on one or during a group meeting.

Providing Feedback for Improvement

It is essential to set expectations, and you need to make sure that you are describing the behavior or action that needs to be improved on.

Describe the impact of the behavior or action has had on the team, the organization, or the project. This is not an attempt to shame the employee, but it is crucial they understand what impacts it had.

Indicate the desired change and manage expectations with the employee. By setting expectations, it will further reinforce with the employee the desire for them to succeed.

When needed coach or have them coached by a subject matter expert, it is essential to understand what the employee's needs are. Ask questions like – "How can I help you?" and "What can we do for you?"

Close the loop by setting the expectations again for the desired behavior – "Let me clarify my expectation." It is essential to set expectations and encourage employees to think outside of the box and if they are unsure about the next steps to come and speak with you.

Things to Avoid

Don't Wait

Don't wait until the last minute to perform a performance review with an employee. You may feel rushed and feel the pressure to get it done. The employee deserves more than something you just threw together.

Provide Insightful Information

Don't have a 10-15-minute performance or evaluation review. This is another example of just not being prepared and not putting any detail into the report.

Be Honest

Not giving negative feedback is more common than you may think. Giving negative feedback is the only way for the employee to know that there is an issue with their performance.

Focus On The Entire Evaluation Period

Using recent behavior as the primary focus of the evaluation instead of the entire performance period should be avoided. It is essential to keep in mind the evaluations usually span over an extended period instead of just what happened last week.

It's Never Personal

Providing feedback should be personal, and it should come directly from you. You should avoid providing feedback from another employee unless you have it in writing.

Address Issues As Needed

Don't let issues pile up and wait for a scheduled evaluation. If there is an issue that is being repeated by the employee or there are multiple concerns do not wait for the evaluation, address your concerns immediately.

10
Team Management

"If everyone is moving forward together, then success takes care of itself."

- Henry Ford

WITH ANY TEAM DYNAMIC, it is essential to make sure you empower them, communicate well, and are setting expectations for the team. Your ability to coordinate and administer a group of individuals is crucial in most management positions. Creating a positive workplace can take any negative perceptions and turn them into a better work environment for everyone.

Getting to know your team is critical and making time for them will motivate your staff when enthusiasm may be lacking. By continuing to evaluate whether the team feels valued by you and the company will allow you to make adjustments as needed. Developing your team is a never-ending ongoing process and one that is necessary and time well spent by any leader.

Effective teams give companies a significant competitive advantage. In a high-functioning team, the sum is truly greater than its parts. Team members not only benefit from each other's diverse experiences and perspectives but also stimulate each other's creativity. The aim and purpose of a team is to perform, get results, and achieve victory in the workplace. The best managers are those who can gather together a group of individuals and mold them into an effective, competent and capable team.

Stages of Group Development

American organizational psychologist Bruce Tuckman (1965) presented a well-known model of group development that is still widely used today. Based on his observations of group behavior in a variety of settings, he proposed a four-stage map of group evolution—also known as the forming-storming-norming-performing model. He later enhanced the model by adding a fifth and final stage—the adjourning phase.

According to this theory, to successfully facilitate a group, the leader needs to move through various leadership styles over time. Generally, this is accomplished by first being more directive, eventually serving as a coach, and later, once the group can assume more power and responsibility for itself, shifting to a delegator role.

While research has not confirmed that this is descriptive of how groups progress, knowing, and following these steps can help groups be more productive. For example, groups that do not go through the storming phase early on will often return to this stage toward the end of the group process to address unresolved issues.

Forming

In the forming stage, the group comes together for the first time. The members may already know each other, or they may be total strangers. In either case, there is a level of formality, some anxiety, and a degree of guardedness as group members are not sure how they will fit into the group or how work will be conducted. "Will I be accepted? What will my role be? Who has the power in this group?"

These are some of the questions participants think about during this stage of group formation. Because of the large amount of uncertainty, members tend to be polite, conflict-avoidant, and observant. They are trying to figure out the "rules of the game" without being too vulnerable. The leadership style during this phase should be a coordinator.

Storming

Once group members feel sufficiently safe and included, they tend to enter the storming phase. Participants focus less on keeping their guard up as they shed social facades, becoming more authentic and more argumentative. Group members begin to explore their power and influence, and they often stake out their territory by differentiating themselves from the other group members rather than seeking common ground.

Discussions can become heated as participants raise contending points of view and values or argue over how tasks should be done and who is assigned to them. It is not unusual for group members to become defensive, competitive, or jealous. Group members may even take sides or begin to form cliques within the group. The leadership style during this phase should be delegator.

Norming

Group members often feel relief at the norming stage, wherein they are much more committed to each other and the group's goal. Group members feel energized and are now ready to get to work. Finding themselves more cohesive and cooperative, participants find it easy to establish their own ground rules (or norms) and define their operating procedures and goals.

The group tends to make big decisions, while subgroups or individuals handle smaller decisions. Hopefully, at this point, the group members are more open and respectful toward each other, and members ask each other for both help and feedback. The leadership style during this phase should be directive.

Performing

Galvanized by a sense of shared vision and a feeling of unity, the group is ready to go into high gear. Members are more interdependent, individuality, and differences are respected, and group members feel themselves to be part of a greater entity. At the performing stage, participants are not only getting the work done, but they also pay more considerable attention to how they are doing it. The leadership style during this phase should be a coach.

Adjourning

Many groups or teams formed in a business context are project-oriented and therefore are temporary. Alternatively, a working group may dissolve due to organizational restructuring. As when we graduate from school or leave home for the first time, these endings can be bittersweet, with group members feeling a combination of victory, grief, and insecurity about what is coming next.

For those who like routine and bond with fellow group members, this transition can be particularly challenging. Group leaders and members alike should be sensitive to handling these endings respectfully and compassionately. An ideal way to close a group is to set aside time to debrief ("How did it all go? What did we learn?"), acknowledge each other, and celebrate a job well done.

Identify Team Roles

It has been identified over there years that there are ten key roles that individuals can take on when working in a group dynamic. It is crucial for leaders to identify and adopt the roles that the employees are taking on. These roles are the core values and behaviors of the employee, and it is not uncommon for an employee to take on more than one team role.

Ineffective leaders might identify an employee with a specific social role and continue to engage the employee with no improvement. This is why it is essential to identify the social functions the employee takes on and is the right person for the right job.

The ten roles are broken down into three different types of roles. These are task roles, social roles, and boundary-spanning roles. Team leadership is effective when leaders can adapt the roles they are contributing or ask others to contribute to what the team needs, given its stage and the tasks at hand.

Task Roles

1. The contractor role includes behaviors that serve to organize the team's work, including creating team timelines, production schedules, and task sequences.

2. The creator role deals mostly with changes in the team's task process structure, such as reframing the team goals and looking at their context.

3. The contributor role is essential, because it brings information and expertise to the team.

4. The completer role is also important, as it transforms ideas into action. Behaviors associated with this role include following up on tasks, such as gathering needed background information or summarizing the team's ideas into reports.

5. The critic role includes "devil's advocate" behaviors that go against the assumptions being made by the team.

Social Roles

1. The cooperator is a proactive role that includes supporting those with expertise related to the team's goals.

2. The communicator role includes behaviors that are targeted at collaboration, such as practicing good listening skills and appropriately using humor to defuse tense situations. Having a good communicator helps the team to feel more open to sharing ideas.

3. The calibrator role is an important one that serves to keep the team on track in terms of suggesting any needed changes to the team's process. This role includes initiating discussions about potential team problems like power struggles or other tensions.

Boundary Spanning Roles

1. The consul role includes gathering information from the larger organization and informing those within the organization about team activities, goals, and successes. Often, the consul role is filled by team managers or leaders.

2. The coordinator role includes interfacing with others within the organization so that the team's efforts are in line with other individuals and teams within the organization.

Foster Trust

Everything about managing your team well depends on earning others' trust in you. If your team is confident that you'll do the right thing as their leader, they will accept your authority and guidance.

When you become a manager, competency is no longer enough—you need to earn people's trust. You have already got to this level, so you were put into leadership because you are known to be a competent employee. Learn the factors that contribute to building trusting relationships.

When Teams Trust Their Leaders

Teams will work better through any disagreements that inevitably arise. Differences are not abnormal in any team; not everyone can agree at all times. What matters is how you and your team moves forward.

The team members work harder both individually and as a team if they trust their leader.

Employees will stay with an organization longer, and they will be more loyal.

Team members will contribute better ideas and more often as they are not afraid to speak up. Leaders will create a positive culture for their employees to feel comfortable to express themselves.

Building Trust Between Members

Trust between members is one of the essential elements of a capable team. When team members trust each other, they are more productive.

Host an off-site Team Meetings

Convene your entire team, including remote members. Time spent together outside the office creates opportunities for team members to get to know one another on a personal level.

Hold Team Lunches

Encourage casual conversation for a half-hour. Prompt team members to reveal a little bit about themselves—their upbringing, families, hobbies, travels. If there is room in the budget, offer to buy the team lunch from time to time. This helps drop some guards as most people enjoy a free lunch.

Add a Personal Touch to Meetings

At the beginning of a meeting, ask each member—those in the room and those joining virtually—to give a brief personal or professional update. Building relationships before the meeting begins and improves communication going forward.

Build Team Cohesiveness

Have team members take a personality test, such as Myers-Briggs, and share the results with the group. Being aware of each other's personality styles helps people feel more comfortable airing conflicts and collaborating.

The fundamental factors affecting group cohesion include the following:

- **Similarity**: The more similar group members are in terms of age, sex, education, skills, attitudes, values, and beliefs, the more likely the group will bond.

- **Stability**: The longer a group stays together, the more cohesive it becomes.

- **Size**: Smaller groups tend to have higher levels of cohesion.

- **Support**: When group members receive coaching and are encouraged to support their fellow team members, group identity is strengthened.

- **Satisfaction**: Cohesion is correlated with how pleased group members are with each other's performance, behavior, and conformity to group norms.

Strengthen Team Identity

Team identity—team members' sense that they share a bond and a purpose are critical for high performance. Being able to have this ability to bring people together around a common mission is a crucial skill a leader must possess and hone.

Benefits of a Team with a Strong Identity

- Teams with a strong identity have a greater willingness to collaborate. The stronger the collaboration the team has, the more productive they are.

- Teams will feel more comfortable sharing information as they have a better understanding of their peers' roles. They also understand that knowledge should not be used as power.

- Teams will display an increased effort and commitment to each other.

- Joint decision making will be displayed, and the team will not feel uncomfortable speaking with each other in group settings.

- Prioritizing team goals ahead of personal goals will be apparent as the team works toward common goals and sets individual goals aside.

Causes of Weak Team Identify

New Teams

It's natural for new teams to suffer from some lack of identity. It is essential to not only understand that but make sure that you are focusing on this for new teams. Try to bring the team together as often as possible and create an environment where they all can feel comfortable to communicate with each other.

New Team Members

When new members join the team after the work has begun, team identity can suffer if the newcomers are disruptive or made to feel like outsiders.

The Diversity of Members

Differing assumptions, cultural backgrounds, and ways of working and thinking can lead to misunderstandings or tensions among members.

Lack of a Shared Sense of Purpose

Without a clear and compelling reason for working together, the individuals who make up a team are likely to put their interests above those of the group.

Rally Your Team

From time to time, you need to rally your team up to accomplish a task, whether that is a project or just dealing with a heavy operational workload.

- Include everyone, make sure that every able individual is present to assist. This helps with team cohesiveness.

- The critical thing when "rallying the troops" is to make sure that your attitude always remains positive.

- Make sure that you have a clear message and also that your directives are understood by the employees.

- Assign a team leader as needed. When delegating work out make sure that you have identified an owner.

- Provide small incentives when you can. Offer an outing to lunch or bring in breakfast or even order a pizza when the task is complete or during the event.

Things to Avoid

Find Your Balance

Not checking in often enough is the flip side to micromanaging. Having an independent team is excellent, but they still need to hear from their manager from time to time. Visit in on them at least once or twice a day.

Using Email Too Much

Relying on email too much for correspondents is also an issue. While most communications can get put into an email, some are done best in person with the team. Set up a meeting with your team and get some good old-fashioned face time in.

Treat Everyone the Same

You need to treat all employees equally. While this seems like another no-brainer, you must make sure they all receive the same equal treatment. This can cause discord in your environment and also create unnecessary employee turnover.

Don't Bully

As a leader, you can intimidate others even if you do not mean to do so. This is another situation where you want to remember your audience. This needs to be taken very seriously, and you could lose your job over this.

Avoid Taboo Subjects

As a leader, you must also make sure that you are curbing discussions surrounding race, religion, and politics. Remind your team that these topics are not meant for the workplace. These topics typically make people feel uncomfortable. Also, as a leader, you should not be using your position as a way to get up on your soapbox and spark debates.

Building Walls

There is such a thing as having a team that is too cohesive. The more strongly members identify with the group, the easier it is to see outsiders as inferior or even (in extreme cases) as enemies. This form of prejudice can have a downward spiral effect. It is important to ensure your team keeps this in check and keeps an open mind.

11
Managing Difficult Employees

"One bad apple can spoil the bunch."

- *Unknown*

THERE IS ONE IS EVERY GROUP, an employee that can be difficult to manage. When you first start working with a new team, this employee may not be easy to recognize; however, once you start working with your team more, it is easy to spot one.

Difficult employees that exhibit lousy behavior can impact your team in many ways. Difficult employees affect morale, productivity, and customer service satisfaction and overall harm the organization.

Depending on the behavior that is exhibited by the employee, the actions that can be taken against them span from education to legal action. Identifying and correcting the bad behavior in employees needs to be taken very seriously by their manager. As a leader, it is your responsibility to ensure that your team's wellbeing, productivity, and performance is protected.

Difficult Employee Types

There are quite a few different employee behavioral types which can be broken down and identified once you understand what you are looking for. Each style of employee that is listed below can have a negative impact on the team in their own unique way. Once you had identified, it is important to focus in on the employee and manage expectations.

The Bully

This employee style is someone that is always being overcritical of others work and directly disagrees with their manager's expectations. They usually can and does do everything in their power to deter the team from reaching their objectives or at the very least slows the team down.

This employee style is toxic to the team, and while constructive criticism should be welcomed, this individual usually crosses a line. Identifying this employee style is generally very easy to spot. If the employee cannot correct this after bringing this to their attention, you need to start considering moving them out of the organization.

The Procrastinator

With all of the work that needs to get done daily, it is not uncommon to get behind from time to time. However, this employee is usually always behind in their work and is continually requires to be micromanaged. Once identified, make sure that you are managing expectations and holding them accountable when tasks or projects are not met.

The Spotlight Seeker

The spotlight seeker is always finding ways to take credit for other employees work. The attention always needs to be on them. This employee style can be a morale killer for other employees if not identified. It is essential to understand what the employees own when they are working as a team to achieve a goal or complete a project.

The Gossip

Some employees love to spread rumors and not only be a part of gossiping; they usually are the ringleaders in most cases. There is no place for this in any work environment and can cause collateral damage to the team and you if you do not correct this. When this identified bring this to the attention of the employee and make sure they understand that this is not acceptable.

The Rebel

It can be stressful enough when a situation at work arises, and you need to delegate an owner, you approach an employee, and they indicate that it is not their job. Perhaps they are even to able to quote their job description.

It is most likely that the employee is disengaged and this needs to be corrected as soon as possible. One way to combat this is to manage expectations for specific situations. It is essential to make sure that the employee understands that certain circumstances warrant requests that may not be in their job descriptions. Job descriptions are more like a guideline and cannot list all the expectations of the company in a few pages.

The Jaded

The jaded employee feels they have given all they can to the company but didn't get anything in return for all of their hard work. The jaded employee is not afraid to let everyone know this and can be very vocal about how the company did not do right by them. This type of employee can be toxic to the environment and may try to have other employees jump on the bandwagon.

If the employee is still engaged, then one way to overcome this is to start to recognize the hard work they are doing. If they are getting up on their soapbox and are badmouthing the company you need to make sure you bring them in your office and explain that this is not tolerated at your company or at any other.

The Whiner

You are almost guaranteed to have one of these employee styles in your team at one point in your career. While some complaints are justified, this employee has to have something or someone to complain about regularly. It can be very frustrating to deal with as a manager as it is critical to listen to your employees but can be challenging to correct.

Remember that if they are complaining to you about something or someone, then they are most likely complaining to the rest of the team about this issue as well. This employee style can take a positive work environment and turn it into a negative one. This is one employee style that reminds us why it is good to work closely with your team.

The Runaway

The runaway is an employee that is never around when you need them. The employee either disappears physically or is not present mentally. Some topics may and can be uninteresting at times during work. However, this is just not acceptable. Bring this to the employee's attention behind closed doors as soon as you notice this.

The Hot Head

This employee has a temper problem and has difficulty controlling their emotions. Some employers allow this type of employee; however, overreacting in the workplace is not acceptable. They usually tend to intimidate others and have no problem verbally attacking those that offended them.

While it is not that uncommon for some employees to lose their cool, it is the repeat offenders that need to be identified. If you notice a trend, it is essential to address this with them and manage expectations. If they are unwilling to listen or seek out support to correct this behavior, it is best to move them out of the organization.

The Super Competitor

There is nothing wrong with healthy competition; however, you will occasionally encounter the super competitor. They usually take the competition to the next level and can cause tension on the team.

By taking things to the next level, it can also cause undue stress on the other workers during team projects. This is a situation that you need to address head-on with the employee. Having this interaction with the employee is very much a tightrope act and is the last thing you want to do to take the wind out of their sails. Be careful when having this conversation.

The Blamer

While it is crucial for some issues or problems to be identified, this employee is usually the first to point fingers. Not only are they continually shifting responsibility, they never taking ownership of an issue or acknowledge that they have made a wrong decision.

The best approach for rectifying this behavior is to approach the employee head one. Sometimes you need to pick your battles, but if the issue is with the employee, they need to understand the mistakes that were made. Making sure they are held accountable is essential.

The Joker

It is always good to bring a bit of levity to most work environments; however, there are some employees take this above and beyond. The joker feels like their primary function is to entertain the team. This style can be counterproductive as it can distract others from doing their duties. Ensure this employee is keeping this in check and ask them to find a balance.

Things to Avoid

Don't Wait

Anytime you see a behavior that needs to be corrected, and you need to focus on fixing that behavior as quickly as possible. If you wait too long, the damage to the team could be too significant and harder to correct the team's course.

Don't Give Up

Working with an employee to correct a bad behavior can take time. It can be frustrating when lousy employee behavior is not fixed in a timely fashion. If you have tried to adjust the bad behavior with the employee and it does not get corrected the first go around, try a different method to fix it. It may take a few attempts to alter the bad behavior that was exhibited by the employee.

Avoiding the Issue

Not taking any action is the worst thing a manager and a leader can do. Never ignore the issue; this will show your team that you are a leader that does not care about their environment. It also demonstrates to the team that you are a leader that does not take action.

Another message you may send to the team is that bad behavior is acceptable in the workplace. By not taking action to attempt to correct the bad behavior could also send your team into a tailspin which could be challenging to recover.

12
Dealing with Employee Conflict

"Don't ever take down a fence until you know why it was put up."

- Robert Frost

IT HAPPENS IN GROUPS BOTH BIG AND SMALL, and it is common to have to deal with employees that do not get along. Employees that are not getting along can be caused by any number of different things, such as personalities to lifestyles to opinions. Conflicts can also create a divide in your team as those that are at ends will most likely try to include other employees.

Employee conflicts can be a drain on the team efficiencies and productivities, and as a manager or leader, it is your responsibility to address it. Disputes cannot go unmanaged as even simple arguments between employees can escalate into more significant issues. Also, if the situation is left unmanaged, it could have damaging impacts such as reduced productivity, the loss of key employees, and the loss of trust in your leadership.

When employee conflicts break out, be prepared to work closely with both employees and or groups. The fact of the matter is employees don't need to be friends, but they do have to work together to get the job done.

Although the word conflict seems to have a negative connotation, not all conflict has a negative result. Functional conflict is the type of conflict that arises when people brainstorm and share good ideas, and positive outcomes come from the conflict. Some leaders encourage substantive conflict by assigning "devil's advocate" roles to team members and inviting those characteristically known as naysayers to meetings.

Types of Conflicts

Intrapersonal Conflict

Intrapersonal conflict arises within a person. Intrapersonal conflict can occur because of differences in roles. A manager may want to oversee an employee's work, believing that such oversight is a necessary part of the job.

The employee, on the other hand, may consider such extensive oversight to be micromanagement or evidence of a lack of trust. Role conflict, another type of intrapersonal conflict, includes having two different job descriptions that seem mutually exclusive. This type of conflict can arise if you're the head of one team but also a member of another group.

Interpersonal Conflict

Interpersonal conflict can occur between coworkers, managers, and employees, or CEOs and their staff. Interpersonal conflict is a key source of stress. In particular, employees who have an agreeable personality and those who have less social support at work report fluctuations in their happiness levels. These levels of happiness are in reaction to how much interpersonal conflict they experience daily.

Competition could be one primary reason behind the interpersonal conflict. Interpersonal conflict can also arise from personality or value differences. For example, one person's style may be to "go with the gut" on decisions, while another wants to make decisions based on facts.

Many companies suffer because of interpersonal conflicts, and keeping conflicts centered around ideas rather than individual differences is vital in avoiding a conflict escalation.

Intergroup Conflict

Intergroup conflict is a conflict that takes place among different groups. Types of groups may include various departments or divisions in a company, an employee union, management, or competing companies that supply the same customers.

Intergroup conflict is often made even worse due to the individual tendency for in-group bias. This may occur in groups that are similar in sex, religion, age, or race, or in groups that are created by organizational structure. The resulting "us versus them" mentality is often the reason behind organizational and international conflict.

How To Handle It

Listen to Both Sides

It is essential to get a full understanding of the situation and to listen to both sides of the argument. Initially, you will want to listen to both sides separately. This will create an environment that they feel comfortable in speaking more freely.

Also, it is important not to take sides initially. Sometimes it is easy to take sides depending on the situation. To take sides, as a leader, you need to be open to discussing this with both parties before jumping to conclusions.

Resolve it quickly

When an employee conflict occurs, do not allow too much time to pass before addressing it with the employees. It is essential to address the concern as soon as possible.

Addressing the situation as quickly as possible also allows the employees to explain the situation better to you. As time passes, the more the story changes. Tensions can increase and fester among the employees, and the situation may get worse.

Encourage Employees to resolve it themselves

Depending on the type of argument, and whether or not Human Resources needs to get involved, leave it up to the employees to resolve their conflicts. The employees need to be given a chance to take ownership of the situation unless the situation warrants immediate action.

Some arguments can be petty like a discussion over a politics or a favorite sports team. Make sure the employees understand that this is up to them to resolve the issue and that arguing at work is not acceptable.

Consult the Employee Handbook

Some arguments can cross the boundaries of what is acceptable in a workplace environment and what is not. If you feel that a line was crossed with one of the employees or both, it is essential to make sure policies are identified and enforced. If it is identified that a policy was broken, you should reach out to your Human Resources department to get involved with the situation.

Teach, Practice, Repeat

As a leader, some situations can be learning ones for the employees. If a conflict occurs and you feel there is a process that can be followed to alleviate tensions work with the employees to coach them on the method or process.

Once you have shown them the process, it is crucial for them to perform it with you in a way that they can practice and have a full understanding. Work with the employee again and again until they feel comfortable performing the process or method.

Change the Composition of the Team

If the conflict is between team members, the easiest solution may be to change the composition of the team. Separating the personalities that were at odds may be a quick fix to the problem.

In instances in which conflict is attributed to the widely different styles, values, and preferences of a small number of members, replacing some of these members may resolve the problem. If that's not possible because everyone's skills are needed on the team, and substitutes aren't available, consider a physical layout solution.

Research has shown that when known antagonists are seated directly across from each other, the number of conflict increases. However, when they are seated side by side, the conflict tends to decrease.

Create a Common Opposing Force

Group conflict within an organization can be mitigated by focusing attention on a common enemy, such as the competition. The "enemy" need not be another company—it could be a concept, such as a recession, that unites previously warring departments to save jobs during a downturn.

Consider Majority Rule

Sometimes a group conflict can be resolved through majority rule. That is, group members take a vote, and the idea with the most votes is the one that gets implemented. The majority rule approach can work if the participants feel that the procedure is fair. It is important to keep in mind that this strategy will become ineffective if used repeatedly with the same members, typically winning.

Organizational Adjustments

If the situation cannot be resolved between the employees and both employees are good workers and suitable for the company, you may want to consider an organizational adjustment.

It is not uncommon to separate workers that cannot get along. Whether that means moving them to another department or having them work on another team, it may be the right thing to do for both them and the company.

Things to Avoid

Avoid Passing the Buck

Do not make an organizational adjustment if the employee is toxic; do not make that employee someone clse's headache. Sometimes if the employee is toxic and has been identified as a repeat offender, then you may way to consider starting the process to move them out of the company.

Do not put the ownership of dealing with an employee conflict on another manager or Human Resources. It is best to handle the situation yourself as you are most likely most familiar with the people and the situation.

Don't Be the Only One Speaking

When speaking with your employees and listening to their side of the employee conflict, don't just wait for your turn to speak, allow them to explain their side of the situation thoroughly.

Never In Public

When confronting an employee do not do it in public, make sure you are having all the conversations behind closed doors. By drawing attention to an issue that an employee has in front of other team members, it sends several different messages, none of which are good ones.

Remove Emotions

Keep emotions out of this. It is essential to remain professional at all times and to keep a level head. Regardless of the situation, you must stay emotionally in control.

13
Dealing with Toxic Environments

"Stay away from negative people. They have a problem for every solution."

- Albert Einstein

A TOXIC ENVIRONMENT can make you feel uncomfortable, unappreciated, or undervalued. This type of environment can come from your boss, your peers, other teams, and your employees. A toxic workplace can not only stifle one's career, but it can also have adverse effects on their health.

While the dangers of a toxic environment are well known, it can be challenging to identify and diagnose. All jobs have some level of stress, even on good days. As a leader in your organization is crucial that you identify the root cause of the toxic environment as quickly as possible.

Identify the Toxic Environment

There are many different red flags you should be looking for when you sense that the workplace environment you are working for is toxic. When it comes to your instincts in this situation, trust them.

If you feel like something is fishy at work, chances are you might be right. It is possible that the toxic environment is being created from the top down or on the other hand, from the bottom up.

As a leader, if you find yourself in a situation where one or more of your employees are creating a toxic environment, it is your responsibility to ensure this is addressed. If you turn a blind eye, you are equally to blame for the toxic environment that is occurring in the workplace.

Lack of Transparency

Sometimes the overall job itself can be difficult, as a leader, providing the proper feedback on how they are performing at their job may be setting them up to fail. Lack of transparency in their job role or communications about their objectives makes it almost impossible to have a mutually respectful, trusting relationship in the workplace.

Another area for lack of transparency can be demonstrated by a lack of communication where employees find out about a decision after it has been implemented. This usually stems from the top down and can cause mass confusion as well as a feeling of disconnect for your team.

Inconsistent Rulebook or Policies

It is crucial for any leader to ensure that the rulebook is being followed. However, when a leader holds one employee accountable but lets another employee get away with the same broken rule or behavior, it comes across as favoritism.

When a company's policies and procedures are not followed, chaos, inconsistency, and poor quality can develop. Customers, vendors, and employees wind up hating dealing with the company and its staff.

You're Being Bullied

With all of the education on this topic, one would think this is a thing of the past. However, it runs rampant in toxic workplaces to this day. Being mistreated by a supervisor or peer is just not acceptable. Any conduct where someone is repeatedly being threatened, humiliated, or intimidated need to be reported immediately.

A Punitive Environment

If you find yourself at work in an environment where you have to keep your head down if you realize that if you make a mistake, criticize or make a suggestion, you get attacked and or punished. This type of environment stifles creativity or innovation and increases worker stress.

Managers are Dictators

Having a dictator of a manager is a red flag that you are working in a toxic environment. A dictator can create an atmosphere of distrust and usually sends morale to an all-time low. This will suck the life out any team and often has high turnover if this is not corrected.

Leadership Doesn't Support You

A good leader should be supporting your ideas, goals, and aspirations. It is not uncommon for leaders to put their interests first. Unfortunately, it is not unusual for some leaders to prevent your growth and prevent you from promotions.

This could be due to jealousy of your performance, and they may start taking credit for your work. This type of behavior, of course, undermines all of the hard work the employees are doing, which should be addressed as soon as possible.

How to Fix a Toxic Workplace

As a leader, you need to ensure that your employees are in an environment in which supports them, encourages them, and is one in which they are productive and happy.

1. Identify Problem Behaviors

There are a number of warning signs that can be easily identified that could be turning your workplace toxic. Some common signs are:

- Gossiping or social cliques

- Bullying Behavior

- Excessive absenteeism, illness or fatigue

- High Turnover

- Imbalanced working conditions such as discriminatory policies or wage gaps

- Unrealistic workloads or deadlines

- Unsafe or morally questionable working conditions

- Everything that you or someone else does is criticized

- Employees are constantly fearing they will get fired

2. Evaluate

Once you have identified some of the behaviors in the workplace, it is time to delve deeper and understand how these behaviors are being supported. You need to look at the company's leadership and its values. If you are new to the leadership role in this environment, it may not always be clear. Be on the lookout for:

- Discriminatory beliefs

- Treating employees as assets, not people

- Information Guarding (Poor Communication or unclear expectations)

- Aggressive or hostile leadership styles

- Lack of Accountability

- Lack of Appreciation or recognition of good work

3. Plan Your Next Steps

Now that you have a clear understanding of the issues, it is now time to start to plan your repair strategy. If there are multiple issues, tackle the most significant problems with the biggest impacts first. It is vital that you:

- Listen to your employees – Set some time aside to ensure that you speak to all employees that are involved.

- Assign realistic workloads and deadlines – Work closer with your employees to understand how long it takes to perform tasks.

- Communicate Transparently – Set and manage expectations with your employees and teams.

- Acknowledge Good Work – Recognize an employee or a team when good work is accomplished or performed.

- Enforce the Rules for all Employees – Ensure that you are not playing favorites and that you have a clear understanding of the company polices so they can be enforced.

4. Implement your Plan

It is now time to execute your plan. At this point, you have identified bad behavior and where it stems from. You have also engaged the employees that are involved. You understand that you need to create realistic workloads, communicate transparently, acknowledge and recognize good work, and enforce all company policies equally.

To execute your plan correctly, you need to make sure that you have created new policies or standard operating procedures as required. Ensure that you have set up regular team meetings and are communicating information to the team. Implementing your strategic plan is as essential, or even more important, than your strategy.

It is also crucial that you are holding all employees responsible and accountable for adhering to any changes you have made. If they fail to do so, you need to understand why and handle accordingly.

5. Reflect and Change As Needed

Any changes, policies, or processes that you have implemented should be given enough time to take root as changes will not happen overnight. It is important that you monitor the progress, and resist the urge to make any changes if only a little time has passed. After a couple of months have passed meet with the individuals you involved and reflect on how things have been going since the last change you have made.

Remember that any changes you have made can be further tweaked, modified, or abolished entirely as you see fit. Culture change is a big undertaking, but if you invest the time to change a toxic environment to a positive one, your teams' productivity will pay dividends.

Things to Avoid

Focus on Solutions Not Complaints

Nothing is more toxic and contagious than employees complaining. Whether it be bad-mouthing each other, company leadership or dress code policies, complaints show a mentality of defeat rather than feeling empowered by the company culture.

Do Not Avoid the Issues

The last thing you want to do is to avoid the issues, especially after being able to identify a problem. Ignoring a matter will not make the situation go away and will most likely make the situation worse over time.

14
Written Corrections

"A coach is someone who can give correction without causing resentment."

- *John Wooden*

WRITING SOMEONE UP is never an easy thing to do, but it is necessary to make sure the employee understands there is an issue. Making sure you are managing expectations for the employee is essential.

Just as recognition is important to reinforce positive behavior if negative behavior has been identified, it is equally important to punish the employee. Expectations must be set for the employee that there are consequences to negative behavior. As a leader, you need to ensure employees understand there are rewards and punishments in the workplace.

When writing an employee up, it is vital that you are not only making sure Human Resources is aware of the situation but that you are also following all the processes that they recommend. Written corrections usually take place after multiple verbal corrections have taken place.

Organizational Behavior Modification

You need to make sure you are making every attempt to modify the behavior of the employee to achieve the expected results. Organizational Behavior Modification or OB Mod is a reinforcement theory to change an employee's behavior in the workforce.

The OB Mod consists of five stages:

Step 1: It is important to identify the behavior that needs to be modified. For example, the employee has a problem with absenteeism.

Step 2: You need to be able to measure the baseline. In the example of the employee dealing with absenteeism, we need to identify how many times the employee has been absent, this week, this month, etc.

Step 3: It is important to analyze the antecedents and outcomes. You need to identify why the employee is absent and what are the impacts and effects on the team and the organization.

During this step you need to also make sure the employee is not being unintentionally rewarded. For example, if the employee is still getting paid or if they are avoiding unpleasant tasks or assignments which are being done by their employees.

Step 4: At this step you need to intervene, and writing up the employee up may be necessary.

Step 5: As a manager you need to make sure you are continually measuring the behavior periodically and is maintained.

It Should Never Be A Surprise

If there is an ongoing issue, the employee should never be surprised. You want to make sure that you have had at the very least, one discussion regarding their performance before writing them up.

There should be constant communications and updates regarding any employee deficiencies. Regular communications should not only be sent to the employee but also all stakeholders, such as your supervisor and HR as needed.

Coaching and opportunities should be extended to the employee, so they have a chance to improve. It is important to remember that writing someone up does not necessarily mean that the employee is on their way out. The message to the employee must remain positive during this process, especially if they are improving.

Never Reprimand an Employee in Public

These conversations should never be in public and should be behind closed doors. Reprimanding an employee in public can create a negative environment.

Include Human Resources

Make sure HR is involved and is aware of the process. It is important to make sure that they are included just in case this situation escalates.

Follow your HR recommendations and processes. Most likely, your organization already has processes and procedures to follow, which will make your job during this process easier. Make sure you are following them

Use Documentation

Ensure you are writing someone up based on a written policy, procedure, or job description. By clearly identifying a policy, procedure, or job description, this will help build a strong case and one that is easy for the employee to understand.

If needed, create a process and procedure then train employees if one does not exist; Ensure the necessary shareholders are involved as required. Once the new process or procedure is created, it is time to make sure all employees are trained and understand the newly created standard.

Include Multiple People

If possible, when having crucial conversations or writing up an employee, try to include your supervisor as well. Sometimes "he said / she said" situations arise and having a third party sit in can verify and bend the scale.

Performance Improvement Plan

Sometimes employees do not improve even after writing them up, ensure that it is recorded and implement a PIP (Process Improvement Plan). A PIP is a written plan to provide the employee with a roadmap to improve in areas they are having difficulties in and sets expectations.

Typical PIPs are usually 90 days and are then discussed with the employee at the end of 90 days. Depending on the situation, you can add or subtract the duration of the PIP.

Keep a lookout for a temporary improvement in productivity and attitude, which is the psychological reaction. The change may be a temporary improvement, so it is essential to monitor this closely. If the employee does not improve, then termination is usually the next step.

Things to Avoid

Stick With the Facts

Keep the personal impressions and conclusions out of the content and remain professional. When writing someone up avoid emotional content.

Spell Out the Consequences

Forgetting to include consequences for undesired behavior is an issue. Clearly outlining the problem and the consequences, so the employee understands what will happen if this action is not corrected is necessary. Setting and managing expectations crucial to this process.

Remain Calm

Do not engage the employee in any heated exchange. Sometimes the employee may respond with anger or blame. Remain calm at all times.

Be Prepared

Not having the proper documentation readily available or having spotty documentation during the event can draw the process out. Make sure you have all necessary documentation that supports the employee being fired as well as all previous verbal warning documentation and prior write-ups.

15
Firing an Employee

"It's better to be alone than in bad company."

- George Washington

FIRING SOMEONE is one of the hardest things that a leader has to do. I have never met a single person that gets some joy out of doing this task. It is one of the necessary functions that a leader must do for the greater good of the organization. If you do not feel that you have it in you to fire someone being in a leadership role may not be best suited for you. You will most likely have to fire someone at least once in a leadership role.

Firing someone usually takes time and is not something most employers can do on a whim. The process of firing someone could take weeks and even months. In most cases, those employees that are poor performers need to have their performance tracked and recorded. Their performance needs to be measured, and they must be provided opportunities to improve.

As you familiarize yourself with the process and procedure, it will get easier. The emotions you may have during the event will lessen over time, and the more you do this, the more comfortable you will become to those events. Again, it is essential to keep in mind that you are doing this for the better good of the organization, and it should never be personal.

Terminating an Employee

Terminating an employee is one of the hardest things to do as a leader. I have never met a leader that enjoyed doing this but is part of the job that is necessary from time to time. If you feel you cannot make those types of decisions, then you shouldn't become a manager. It is a harsh reality that you will eventually have to make a difficult decision that can be life-altering for the employee.

Do What is Right for the Company

It is crucial for you as a leader to do what is right for the company. While it is essential to make sure the employee is happy and productive, it is equally important to ensure that the employees are performing their job as needed.

If the employee is not performing up to par, and you have tried to improve their productivity. If you do not see any improvement, it may be time to let the employee go. Keep in mind that if the company fails, everyone is out of a job. There should really be no room in a company for those that cannot keep with the recommended minimum tasks.

Only Terminate an Employee When all else Fails

Coach, Coach, Coach! Make sure that they have been given every opportunity to succeed. Do not give up on the employee, remember, part of your role is to make sure your employees succeed.

If terminating an employee is unavoidable, push the employee out of the company rather than to another department. Transferring them to another department is not fair to the leadership of that area or the organization.

Follow the process!

Make sure that you are following any rules and processes, and keep in mind that HR is there to help, reach out to them as needed. Ensure all discrepancies are documented and submitted. You need to make sure that there is a record of all the issues you have experienced with the employee. This will not only build a stronger case for you; it will also ensure that you are protecting the organization.

Get Human Resources Involved

Make sure HR is in the room when someone is getting fired. It is also essential that there is at least one other person in the room, such as another manager or your supervisor.

Having multiple individuals in the room can prevent any he said, she said situations. It is not uncommon for employees to attempt to protect themselves at all costs as their job in most cases and their livelihood. Having someone in the room with you can back up how the situation went.

In rare cases, it can get physical, and it's always good to have another person in the room. If you feel that a physical altercation may occur with the employee and you have a security team, it is good to have them on standby and are aware of the situation beforehand.

Do It behind Closed Doors

Just like reprimanding someone, never fire anyone in public or in front of other employees. It is essential for employees to feel comfortable in their work environment.

Unless it is unavoidable, never fire someone over the phone, face to face is best. While it may be uncomfortable, it is important to respect the employee even if they are on their way out.

Do Not Draw It Out – Be Direct

Explain why they are being terminated (which should never be a surprise). Be clear and concise with your message and avoid going off on a tangent.

Have them sign off on any paperwork as needed. It is not uncommon for an employee to have to sign off on any confidentiality agreements or other organizational agreements. Make sure you understand the documents just in case they have any questions about them.

Collect any equipment from them, access badge, keys, etc. Make sure you do this immediately after firing someone as you may never see the items again. Escort them off of the property or if needed have security assist. Do not allow the employee to roam and spend too much time speaking with people before they leave. You may find yourself in the middle of a scene you do not want to be part of.

Things to Avoid

Push Them Out

Pushing a poor performer to another department, don't give someone else your headache. It is always best to move poor performers out of your organization.

Keep a Record and Communicate

Don't fire an employee without warning. They should never feel blindsided when it comes down to terminating them, and it is not uncommon to have repeat offenders regardless of the situation, make sure you are keeping a record and communicating and writing up the employee when an infraction occurs.

Collect All Company Property

In most cases, you should not allow the employee to leave until collecting all company property. You may never see that property back again.

Fire Them Yourself

Don't get someone else to do the dirty work. If it is your employee and they report to you, you should be the one to explain why they are being terminated.

This is Not Personal

You need to keep emotions and personal beliefs out of this. Don't allow this to become personal, and it is important to keep in mind this is just about business. Do not get defensive or engage in arguing with them.

16
Recognition

"People work for money, but go the extra mile for recognition, praise, and rewards."

- *Dale Carnegie*

THERE ARE A FEW THINGS that are more important to an employee's morale than recognition. Employees that are recognized are happier when you recognize how much of an impact they have on the team and for the organization. As a leader, it is crucial that you create a culture of appreciation through recognition in your environment.

There is a strong connection between recognition and job satisfaction and leaders that recognize employees create strong bonds with their employees. This not only has positive impacts on the leader and the employee receiving the recognition, but it also affects peers who see good work being rewarded.

Creating an environment where an employee feels valued is one of the best ways to boost morale. If your company does not have a recognition program, work with either your Human Resource department or your fellow leaders as this will pay off with dividends.

Why is Recognition Important at Work?

Recognition communicates to employees that the work they do is valuable and appreciated. It drives more significant levels of discretionary effort, and your employees are inspired and willing to do more.

Usually nothing more than words of encouragement and feedback is needed to strengthen employee behaviors. However, more tangible rewards such as prizes, awards, and ceremonies can help reinforce desirable behaviors.

Encouragement is most effective when it is given immediately after an employee successfully accomplishes a certain task. This why it is important to have a spot rewards program, which awards employees, "on the spot" when they do something particularly well. The awards can consist of cash, gift cards, time off, or anything else employees' value.

Recognition also drives employee retention and talent. It is crucial to have loyal employees as they are the future of your company. Recognition reinforces the organization's values by identifying behavior that is in alignment with those values.

What can you recognize?

- Extra effort – presenting, taking on a project, helping a co-worker or another department.

- Any type of improvements that they recommend that is going to be implemented.

- Accomplishments that they have achieved which can either be personal or work-related.

- Tenure is a common one to celebrate, it also sends a good message to new employees that you appreciate loyalty.

- Birthdays are a good way to recognize your employees, do it with a lunch, a birthday cake or a celebration after work. Make sure to invite all employees!

- If available, give the employees a choice over rewards. Allowing them to provide feedback on what rewards are important to them is a great way to boost morale.

How to Recognize Performance

- Sometimes just saying thank you is enough to boost the employee's spirits.

- Know enough about employees as individuals so you may make the recognition most meaningful for them. i.e., Public versus Private, Oral versus Written

- Written notes (handwritten are more powerful). Send them to their home, so their family sees

- Make recognition a regular agenda item and perform it on quarterly, bi-annual or annual basis.

- Include family members when appropriate, having recognition for the employee not only shows them that you appreciate them, it also shows their family how important that employee is to the company or organization.

- Consider implementing a "Clutch" Award or something that recognizes a highly valued behavior.

- Use storytelling to share recognition with others in the organization.

- Consider that highly motivated employees are often rewarded by being given more challenging, high impact assignments and opportunities to experience professional development and visibility.

- Be sure to use the mechanisms already in place such as "Employee of the Quarter," "Wow" or "Bravo" type programs, Innovator's Award, Employee Referral. Make these more meaningful by adding additional words of recognition.

- Recognize team achievements through internal employee communications such as newsletters as well as the local community newspaper.

Things to Avoid

Reward Those Who Deserve It

Do not award someone for an issue or problem they have caused. It is always essential to understand the root cause. It is important to remember that not everyone gets recognized unless they meet specific criteria.

Broadcast

Try not to recognize achievements with just the employee alone. While you can let them know face to face, it is essential to broadcast to the organization or during a meeting and treat it as a win for the team.

Know Your Employees

There is a flip side to recognizing and broadcasting achievements. If you know the employee is an introvert and does not want to have, the success aired to the entire organization. Send it out to a select few and recognize that individual in private.

Be Consistent

Make sure the recognition is consistent. If the employee recognition is inconsistent, for example, you recognize one employee one month for a win, but then another employee does it a month later, and you do not recognize them, it can come across as favoritism.

Be Specific

Avoid only rewarding outcomes and goal achievement. It is vital to recognize specific behaviors and performance. Make sure you are acknowledging effort as well as actual success.

17
Managing Generations

"Each generation goes further than the generation preceding it because it stands on the shoulders of that generation. You will have opportunities beyond anything we've ever know."

- *Ronald Reagan*

UNDERSTANDING THE GENERATIONAL GAPS between employees has been identified in recent years as an essential area of focus. While we will speaking in generalizations in this section, we do understand that each employee is unique and do not always fall into specific categories.

For the first time in history, five generations will be working side by side. It is essential to understand the generational gaps. Finding motivation differs for someone older to someone younger. It is also critical for a leader to be able to relate to different age groups. Lastly, you will want to encourage employees from different generations to share their knowledge.

Keep in mind that each generation brings with them a different set of skills, attitudes, and capabilities to a role. Managers overall need to be more flexible regarding their management style and change the way they communicate with their employees.

Over the next 30 years, 76 million baby boomers will retire, but there will only be 46 million new workers from Generations X and Y entering the labor force. This demographic trend creates both challenges and opportunities for organizations.

Defining Generations

Each generation can be defined by meeting specific criteria and label certain age groups. The groups listed in this chapter are ones that are identified in the United States. The generational grouping listed in this chapter does not apply to other regions or countries in the world.

The Silent Generation or Traditionalists

In most cases, this generation was too young to see action in World War II, and they were too old to participate in the fun of the Summer of Love. This generation believed that if you followed the rules and worked hard that you would be able to succeed and live the American Dream.

- Born 1928 – 1945

- Silents are considered among the most loyal workers.

- They are highly dedicated and the most risk-averse.

- Their values were shaped by the Great Depression, World War II, and the postwar boom years.

- Silents possess a strong commitment to teamwork and collaboration and have high regard for developing interpersonal communications skills.

The Baby Boom Generation

The boomers were born during an economic and baby boom following World War II. Vietnam War was a reality for this generation. They not only protested the Vietnam War but also participated in the civil rights movement. Rock and Roll played a considerable influence culturally for this generation.

- Born 1946 – 1964

- Boomers are the first generation to declare a higher priority for work over personal life actively.

- They generally distrust authority and large systems.

- Their values were shaped primarily by a rise in civil rights activism, Viet Nam, and inflation.

- They are more optimistic and open to change than the prior generation, but they are also responsible for the "Me Generation," with its pursuit of personal gratification, which often shows up as a sense of entitlement in today's workforce.

Generation X

They were initially called the baby busters because fertility rates fell after the boomers. As teenagers, they experienced the AIDS epidemic and the fall of the Berlin Wall. Sometimes called the MTV Generation, the "X" in their name refers to this generation's desire not to be defined.

- Born 1965 – 1980

- Generation Xers are often considered the "slacker" generation.

- They naturally question authority figures and are responsible for creating the work/life balance concept.

- Born in a time of declining population growth, this generation of workers possesses strong technical skills and is more independent than the prior generations.

- Gen Xers are willing to develop their skill sets and take on challenges and are perceived as very adaptive to job instability.

The Millennial Generation

They experienced the rise of the Internet, September 11th, and the wars that followed. Sometimes called Generation Y because of their dependence on technology. They are viewed to be entitled and narcissistic by other generations.

- Born 1981- 1997

- This group is the first global-centric generation, having come of age during the rapid growth of the Internet and an increase in global terrorism.

- They are among the most resilient in navigating change while deepening their appreciation for diversity and inclusion.

- The Millennials are also the most educated generation of workers today.

- They represent the most team-centric generation since the Silents.

Generation Z

With Generation Z entering the workforce, they are the first generation in history to work along the side of four other generations. It is essential to start to get to know some traits of the next generation in the workforce.

This generation was the firstborn with the Internet and are suspected to be the most individualistic and technology-dependent generation. Sometimes referred to iGeneration or iGen and Post Millennials.

- Born 1998 – 2010

- They seem to be more private than the previous generation the Millennials. As an example, apps like Snapchat and Whisper have seen explosive growth where Facebook has lost 25 percent of this demographic since 2011.

- They are multi-taskers and are taking it to the next level. They prefer to work on four computer screens not two like the millennials.

- They are technology-reliant; this one won't surprise you. Millennials are addicted to technology, get ready for more of the same as Generation Z. In surveys, they put technology in the same category as air and water.

- They are the first generation that cannot remember a time without the internet and spend most of their time on it. What is surprising though is that 72% of Gen Z's prefer to have face to face conversations.

Generation Alpha

Born beginning in 2010, the same year Apple debuted the iPad, these children are more comfortable swiping a tablet or speaking to a voice assistant than most of their adult relatives.

- Born 2010 – TBD

- They will be more self-sufficient, better educated and prepared for big challenges. Gen Alpha will have to take on many of the biggest challenges of the world.

- They will be the most tech savvy and not know a world without social networking. Alpha's will be introduced to mobile phones before becoming teenagers and will take most of the technology we use today for granted.

- Their mobile phones will be so sophisticated when they become teenagers that they will primarily use their phone over a laptop or desktop computer.

Understanding and Managing by Generation

Communication

- Silents and Baby Boomers may appreciate verbal communication about changes in policy or procedures.

- Generation Xers and Millennials may prefer the use of e-mail, instant messages, or corporate broadcasts.

Attractions

- As more Silents retire, Baby Boomers seek

"Postretirement careers."

- Gen Xers demand challenging but balanced work assignments
- Millennials and Generation Z's expect big perks in exchange for loyalty and are technologically savvy. Leaders must find creative ways to recruit and retain talent.

Mentoring Generations

Consider various mentoring models—one-on-one sessions, group programs, senior leadership discussion panels, and a "speed mentoring" program where employees sit across from company experts to ask questions.

No matter what method you choose, making mentoring a part of the employment lifecycle will ensure that the company's history and knowledge continue from one generation to the next. Keep in mind the manager styles, as they are the same regardless of the generation you come from, and that very few managers or leaders are just one style overall.

Silents

For Silents, mentoring was an obligation—they were the senior leaders who were asked to step up as mentors and were happy to do so.

Baby Boomers

Baby Boomers were the generation seeking out mentorship, which led them to view mentoring as a way to get ahead.

Gen Xers

Generation X started pushing Baby Boomers to experiment with virtual relationships and electronic communication. Gen X wanted to engage in more virtual mentoring, and they also want to collaborate more efficiently with their peers.

Millennials

For Millennials, mentoring is merely collaborative, and networked learning that includes many people. It is a process where they use technology to connect with people across an organization so that they can share critical knowledge and skills, and solicit advice and opinions from people with diverse backgrounds.

Millennials determine their goals and developmental needs, and then pair them with older, more experienced employees to create a cross-organizational dialogue among generations.

Generation Z

It is important to remember that Generation Z's are digital natives. With this generation, they do not know a world without the internet. In many cases, they grew up with an iPad or another tablet in hand. In most cases, they are connected with their peers all day every day.

Gen Z'ers expect the workplace to conform to their needs. They are similar to millennials in this way and are relatively identical to boomers as well. This attitude is affecting the workplace.

Generation Alpha

The business world will be confronted with the most demanding customers and employees in history, expecting speed, responsiveness, and customization as a standard: an app-style service from any business they choose to have a relationship with.

As employees, Alphas will be tougher to keep motivated and challenged. In response, many types of work will become more like a series of individual projects and challenges with their rewards.

Things to Avoid

Avoid Blanket Stereotypes

Understand that even though there are certain traits for each generation, it is important to remember that your employees are individuals and do not necessarily always fall into categories or have specific characteristics.

The More Things Change, The More They Stay The Same

Keep in mind that new generations will encounter some of the same issues their older counterparts have faced when entering the workforce. It is important not to overanalyze be overly romantic or too critical about new generations.

Personalize your Approach

As a leader, you will most likely have multiple generations working in your team. It is crucial to understand and recognize that different generation has different needs. Ignoring these differences can cause resentment and discord.

SECTION FOUR

UNDERSTAND YOUR ROLE

Role (Noun) rōl - A function or part performed especially in a particular operation or process

Synonyms: business, capacity, function, job, part, place, position, purpose, task, work;

18
Implementing Change

"Change can be frightening, and the temptation is often to resist it. But change almost always provides opportunities – to learn new things, to rethink tired processes, and to improve the way we work."

- *Klaus Schwab*

CHANGE MANAGEMENT is another problematic area for leaders to overcome. Change management can be as tense a situation as writing someone up or firing someone. Change is inevitable in any environment, whether it is strategic, leadership, or technological changes. It is essential to be cautious when discussing the change with employees.

Communicating change needs to be done formally with your employees. Through proper communication, it will, in turn, tell them why the change is happening, what they should expect, and how the change will benefit them. It is essential to keep employees involved from the start to help with a smooth transition.

Ultimately people fear the unknown and can be initially resistant to it. However, over time, by keeping the communication open it will help build trust with your team. Change management can be challenging, and it is essential to understand how to handle the change and understand what the employee may be thinking and or feeling.

Change is the work of leaders. In today's world, business-as-usual thinking is unacceptable, and exemplary leaders know that they must transform the way things are done. Delivering results beyond expectations can't be achieved with good intentions. People, processes, systems, and strategies all need to change. In addition, all change requires that leaders actively seek ways to make things better—to grow, innovate, and improve.

There is a clear connection between challenge and change; and there's a clear connection between challenge and being an effective leader. The more frequently people see their leader searching outside the formal boundaries of his or her organization for innovative ways to improve, the more strongly they agree that their leader is effective.

Leaders want to make something happen, and are often frustrated by the "if it ain't broke, don't fix it" mentality. They earn the respect of the people around them when they question the status quo, come up with innovative ideas, follow through with the changes they suggest, get feedback, understand their mistakes, and learn from failures.

Passionate and purposeful leadership is particularly important in times of high uncertainty. When risk and complexity increase, people are in greater need of direction and guidance than when times are safer and simpler.

People need a reason to keep on climbing, to keep on striving, to keep on struggling. That reason needs to be more than a short-term reward. It needs to be something more sustaining. When challenging people to grow, innovate, and improve, explain how it will benefit their colleagues, their customers, their families, and their communities. Connect the challenge to the greater good. Give them a reason to care.

Creating Culture Change

There are a few steps that can be followed to change the culture in your organization successfully. Changing a company's culture may be the key to the company's turnaround if there is a mismatch between an organization's values and the demands of its environment.

Communicate Effectively

It is essential to keep the message consistent whenever a change is discussed, so the same message is presented. An example of this would be to have too many separate meetings with employees which may convey different understandings of the change.

Be transparent if possible, call a meeting to break the message with the team and then have a follow-up meeting to discuss the details. For a change effort to be successful, it is essential to communicate the need for change to employees. One way of doing this is to create a sense of urgency on the part of employees and explain to them why changing the fundamental way in which business is done is so important.

Encourage Initiative in Others

Change requires leadership and every person, down to the most junior member of the organization, can drive innovation and improvements in a team's processes. Leaders scize the initiative themselves and encourage initiative in others. They want people to speak up, offer suggestions for improvement, and be straightforward about their constructive criticism.

The more frequently direct reports indicated their leaders "challenge people to try out new and innovative ways to do their work," the stronger were their feelings of accomplishment and belief that they were making a difference.

Change Key Players

A leader's vision is an essential factor that influences how things are done in an organization. Thus, culture change often follows changes at the highest levels of the organization. Moreover, to implement the change effort quickly and efficiently, a company may find it helpful to remove managers and other strategic employees who are acting as a barrier to change.

Role Model

Role modeling is the process by which employees modify their own beliefs and behaviors to reflect those of the leader. The ultimate goal is that these behaviors will trickle down to lower-level employees. When positive role-modeling is executed at top levels, it is likely to have a positive impact on the company culture.

The more people observe their leaders as role models for taking initiative, testing skills and abilities, and learning from experience, the more favorably they feel about their workplaces. By observing exemplary behaviors, people can gain insights into the dynamic nature of the skill they are trying to acquire. Positive role models are necessary because it is impossible for anyone to excel based upon a negative. You can only excel to a positive example.

Train

Well-crafted training programs may be instrumental in bringing about culture change by teaching employees new norms and behavioral styles. Customer reports have been overwhelmingly positive in stores that underwent this training.

Change the Reward System

The criteria with which employees are rewarded and punished have an influential role in determining cultural values. Rewarding employees who embrace the company's new values and even promoting these employees, organizations can make sure that changes in culture have a lasting impact.

Create New Symbols and Rituals

The success of the culture change effort may be increased by developing new rituals, symbols, and stories. By replacing the old ones, new symbols and stories will help enable a culture change and ensure that the new values are communicated.

Layers of Organizational Capacity for Change

Organizational capacity for change (OCC) can be conceptualized as the overall capability of an organization to either adequately prepare for or respond to an increasingly unpredictable and volatile environmental context.

The concept of organizational capacity can be broken down into eight separate and distinct layers. Four of the layers focus on critical human capital and four focus on social infrastructure.

Trustworthy Leaders

No lasting, productive change within an organization ever happens without a modicum of trust between its members. Consequently, the first essential dimension for OCC is the extent to which an organization is perceived to be led by trustworthy leaders.

Trustworthiness can be thought of as the quality of someone being competent and benevolent so that others can safely be in partnership with that person. As Brian Tracy suggests earlier, trustworthiness is important to all human relationships, but it is essential for leadership effectiveness and the ability to prepare for and drive organizational change.

An excellent metaphor the importance of benevolence is that of a knife. Knives are tools that can be handled with great skill, such as preparing food for a meal or defending from an attack. However, if the followers turn the knife over to the leader, they first want to be sure that the leader will not use the knife on them. The knife is a metaphor for power, and leadership involves the proper use of power. All knife-wielding leaders need to show that they know how to use a knife, and that they will not use that knife against their followers.

Trusting Followers

Leaders are only half of the equation when it comes to organizational change; the other half is the followers. This is an individual who is perceived to be competent in leading an organization and who is also perceived as someone who has the best interests of the organization as his or her priority.

Capable Champions

Individuals, and hence organizations, tend to be inertial. In other words, change takes extra energy, and it is much easier to keep doing things how we are accustomed to. Consequently, organizations must identify, develop, and retain a cadre of capable change champions to lead the change initiatives.

Involved Middle Management

Middle managers are those who link top executives to frontline workers. Department heads are classic examples of middle managers, but there are many other types of linkages. While change champions often come from the middle management ranks, middle managers can passively or actively block change initiatives due to their unique position within an organization.

Systems Thinking

These are the rules, structural arrangements, and budgetary procedures that facilitate or hinder an organization-wide—as opposed to a segmental approach to organizational change. While a segmental approach works quite well for routine procedures, it is anathema to the study of nonroutine events such as strategic decision making, organizational change, or both.

Communication Systems

Communication systems involve such things as e-mail networks, face-to-face meetings, telephone calls, and corporate announcements. All of these communication systems are focused on the conveyance of the value for and the means for implementing a proposed organizational change. Organizational change requires reflection and action.

Accountable Culture

While individuals need autonomy in today's organizations to pursue innovative new ideas, they need to be held accountable for delivering results on time and within budget. At the very least, they need to explain the failure to honor deadliness, resource constraints, or both.

Innovative Culture

Innovation culture is the work environment that leaders cultivate to nurture unorthodox thinking and its application. Workplaces that foster a culture of innovation generally subscribe to the belief that change is not the province of top leadership but can come from anyone in the organization. Innovation cultures are prized by organizations that compete in markets defined by rapid change; maintaining the status quo is insufficient to compete effectively, thus making an innovation culture essential for success.

The Seven Stages of Grief

Change can be so difficult for most people that they go through the seven stages of grief. It is important to remember this when evoking significant changes with an individual or group of employees. Depending on the employee, they may go through this very quickly, or it may take some time depending on the individual.

7 Stages of Grief Model

1. **SHOCK & DENIAL -** The employee will probably react to learning of this change with numbed disbelief. They may deny the reality of the change at some level. Shock provides emotional protection from being overwhelmed all at once.

2. **PAIN & FRUSTRATION -** As the shock wears off, it is replaced with the suffering pain. It may make them feel sick to their stomach or give them headaches. They may start to become frustrated with the loss of control over the situation.

3. **ANGER & BARGAINING -** Frustration gives way to anger, and they may lash out and lay unwarranted blame. This is a time for the release of bottled up emotion.

4. **"DEPRESSION," REFLECTION, LONELINESS -** This is a normal stage of grief, and encouragement from others may not be helpful during this stage.

5. **THE UPWARD TURN -** Physical symptoms lessen, and your "depression" begins to lift slightly.

6. **RECONSTRUCTION & WORKING THROUGH -** As they become more functional, their mind starts working again, and they can start seeing the bigger picture. Logic begins to regain a footing.

7. **ACCEPTANCE & HOPE** - During this, the last of the seven stages, you learn to accept and deal with the reality of your situation. Acceptance does not necessarily mean instant happiness. You will find a way forward.

How to Respond to Some Employee Emotions

Denial

Behaviors to expect to see	Actions to Help the Employee
Flip attitude	1. Share accurate information again and again;
Indifferent Talk	2. Ask questions;
Evasion	3. Explain the change and the reasons;
Skepticism	4. Give examples of peers who are changing, learning;
Refusal to Accept the Situation	5. Provide examples of the need for this new system / approach / technology;

Anger

Behaviors to expect to see	Actions to Help the Employee
Grumbling	1. Listen;
Irritation	2. Acknowledge anger;
Mistakes	3. Do not talk them out of it;
Passive-Aggressive	4. Do not assume blame for their anger;
Foot-Dragging	5. In rare cases, if real harm is possible, consult security / ER experts.

Bargaining

Behaviors to expect to see	Actions to Help the Employee
Trying to get out of the situation Make it Go Away Making a Deal or Promise Negotiation	1. Keep the realistic plan in sight; 2. Don't be influenced by promises or negotiations; 3. Reinforce the situation as it is; 4. Gently remind them of reality;

Sadness

Behaviors to expect to see	Actions to Help the Employee
Silence Disheartened Fearful Crying	1. Acknowledge; 2. Sympathize; 3. Encourage talking and sharing feelings either 1:1 or in a supportive group; 4. Probe with questions to understand; 5. Refer to a professional;

Anxiety

Behaviors to expect to see	Actions to Help the Employee
Stressed Spreading Rumors Nervous Productivity lowered	1. Understand and acknowledge the feelings of loss, even if they seem like overreactions. 2. Encourage talking and listen carefully; 3. Do not talk them out of feelings, but offer a different point of view if you have one. 4. Give positive feedback on their progress, if genuine.

Depression

Behaviors to expect to see	Actions to Help the Employee
Downcast Signs of Fatigue Despair Ineffectiveness	1. Empathize and reach out; 2. Initiate conversation and ask questions to draw them out. 3. Promote supportive group events or interaction, impromptu fun.

7 Strategies for Overcoming Resistance to Change

1. **Structure the team to maximize its potential** - Give team members appropriate roles and responsibilities that use skills to their best advantage, while also providing the potential for personal and team development.

2. **Set challenging, achievable, and engaging targets** - Be clear in setting expectations about goals and objectives. Break change projects into smaller milestones, and celebrate achievements. Goals should be seen as progressive and in line with values and beliefs.

3. **Resolve conflicts quickly and effectively** - Utilize the seven methods of care-fronting to regulate and control communicative breakdowns. Encourage openness and honesty and engender an environment of mutual trust and respect.

4. **Show passion** - Communicate passionately and be an example of belief in what the future vision may bring. It is also important to remain positive.

5. **Be persuasive** - Engage employees in change by being an energized leader. Focus on opportunities and persuade rather than assert authority. Share experiences as you influence change through stories that focus on positive change.

6. **Empower innovation and creativity** - Give opportunities for feedback and remain flexible as you alter course toward your change goals. Encourage people to be creative, discover solutions to unfolding problems, and to become part of the change process. The process is complicated for everyone involved, and your team will be more invested with solutions they have created themselves, rather than those dictated to them.

7. **Remain positive and supportive** - People find change unsettling, even though change is a constant in personal lives as well as professional environments. They will need the support of a confident leader who inspires free thought, honest communication, and creativity as individual and team development is encouraged.

Things to Avoid

Things You Should Never Say

Top 5 Things you should never say when discussing the change with an employee.

1. "I have no idea why *they* are making this change."

2. "Well…there is nothing we can do about it- we just need to go along with it."

3. "This is yet another example that they have no idea what we do out here on the floor."

4. "I agree with you, and I don't like it either."

5. "In all my years…this has got to be the stupidest decision *they* have ever made."

Be Clear

Not communicating or articulating the need for a change can confuse your employees. Make sure your team understands the reason behind the change.

Have A Plan

Not having an action plan or providing your employees a roadmap is another way to confuse employees. Without clear direction, your change management initiative could go nowhere.

Shotgun Management

The shotgun management style is a type of management which is characterized by frequent and massive changes, without really understanding what the results may be.

There is nothing wrong with trying something new or trying to change a process; however, doing this too frequently could cause confusion and chaos in your environment.

Pay Attention

During a change, employees may be feeling stressed and anxious about their job security. If the manager, not recognizing this, gives a lot of technical details about the timing and logistics of the change or how the change will benefit the organization, it may result in mistrust in management as the employees' feelings of anxiety are not being recognized and addressed.

Talk the Walk and Walk the Talk

When the behavior from leaders within an organization is inconsistent with the change vision, then all other forms of communication are disregarded. "Walking the talk" is an essential part of the communication system within an organization.

Don't Just Communicate Your Message Once

A change message must be repeated many ways in many different contexts using multiple communication channels. However, this does not mean that daily e-mails with the same message need to be sent out to the entire organization. It does mean that creative and different versions of the same message need to be distributed periodically in various channels. For example, the change vision could be communicated to large and small groups in formal and informal ways at the launch of a major change program.

19
Project Management

"Those who govern, having much business on their hands, do not generally like to take the trouble of considering and carrying into execution new projects. The best public measures are therefore seldom adopted from previous wisdom, but forced by the occasion."

- *Benjamin Franklin*

AS A LEADER IN ANY ORGANIZATION, the job is not just about managing people and day to day operations it is also about managing projects. Regardless of the size of the project, it is essential to stay organized and keep the project on track.

Projects in and out of themselves can be very stressful for not only you as a leader but also for your team. There are numbers of different ways to tackle and approach a project. Over time you will find what works best for you that will help you manage, keep track, and organize your projects.

Excellent project management is about delivering on time, budget, and scope. It is about uniting your ream and being able to create a clear vision for success and gets everyone on the same page. When projects are correctly managed, there is a positive impact that reverberates throughout your team and your organization.

P-O-L-C Framework

The P-O-L-C framework, which stands for Planning, Organizing, Leading, and Controlling, has been a prevalent structure for over a century. This structure has stood the test of time and is the basis for successfully executing projects and can be used in any organization.

Below is an overview of the P-O-L-C chart. These following areas need to be continuously monitored throughout the projects lifecycle as you will need to adapt to changing environments and situations continually.

Planning	Organizing	Leading	Controlling
1. Vision & Mission	1. Organization Design	1. Leadership	1. Systems/Processes
2. Strategizing	2. Culture	2. Decision Making	2. Strategic Human Resources
3. Setting Goals & Objectives	3. Social Networks	3. Communications	
		4. Groups/Teams	
		5. Motivation	

Planning

A successful leader must set objectives to determine the course of action necessary to achieve those objectives. Managers must be aware of environmental conditions and be able to forecast future decisions as well as being good decision-makers.

The first step in the planning process begins with environmental scanning. Project managers must establish objectives, which are statements of tangible actions that need to be achieved, and a timeline for their completion.

Project Manager must then identify alternative courses of action for achieving objectives. After evaluating the various alternatives, planners must make decisions about the best courses of action for achieving goals.

Organizing

Organizing is the function of management that involves developing an organizational structure and allocating human resources to ensure the accomplishment of objectives. The structure of the organization is the framework within which effort is coordinated.

Decisions must be made about the duties and responsibilities of individual jobs, as well as how the responsibilities should be carried out. There are many different ways to departmentalize, including organizing by function, product, geography, or customer.

Leading

If managers are effective leaders, their subordinates will be enthusiastic about exerting effort to attain organizational objectives. To become effective at leading, managers must first understand their subordinates' personalities, values, attitudes, and emotions.

Controlling

Controlling involves ensuring that performance does not deviate from standards. Controlling consists of three steps, which include (1) establishing performance standards, (2) comparing actual performance against standards, and (3) taking corrective action when necessary.

The managerial function of controlling should not be confused with control in the behavioral or manipulative sense. This function does not imply that managers should attempt to manage or to manipulate the personalities, values, attitudes, or emotions of their subordinates.

Two traditional control techniques are budget and performance audits. An audit involves an examination and verification of records and supporting documents. A budget audit provides information about where the organization is with respect to what was planned or budgeted. Whereas a performance audit might try to determine whether the figures reported are a reflection of actual performance.

Although controlling is often thought of in terms of financial criteria, managers must also control production and operations processes — procedures for delivery of services, compliance with company policies, and many other activities within the organization.

Areas of Focus

Get Organized and Stay Organized

Develop an Effective Filing System

While paperwork is unavoidable in most projects as some information does require signatures, it is essential to keep it organized.

Create a folder or binder for all critical paperwork if you must keep them as a hard copy. If possible scan all paperwork and create a filing structure on a computer and save all correspondence in the folder as well.

Create Specific Spreadsheets & Documents As Needed

There is no need to reinvent the wheel. Use templates that you may have used on other projects.

Scour the web for templates that others have created to assist with project management.

Checklists are also a great way to identify who owns a specific task and whether or not it has been completed.

Use Project Management Software

If you have a budget for software, use it! There is plenty of excellent project management software out there.

Do yourself a favor, stick with a name brand. Unless someone highly recommends software stick with a reputable company and some software can be a waste of time and money.

Ultimately, Use What Work for You

Use tools that work for you, whether that is a computer, tablet, phone, pen or paper, post-it notes, etc. You know yourself better than anyone else, utilize what you feel comfortable using. You don't need to have the most expensive equipment out there if you don't feel comfortable using it a pen and notepad work just as well.

Define the Goals and Objectives

It is essential to make sure that you are defining the scope of work early on in the project and are also setting expectations with your teams and stakeholders.

- Make sure you understand what the expected outcome or output of the project.

- Determine any costs and budgets associated with the project.

- Understanding the timeframe and deadlines that you need to meet to complete the project

- Determine the available resources you have about such as employee resources and financial resources

- Break down the tasks into smaller subgroups before tasking to anyone any objectives. This will help the team member met milestones.

Identify Team Strengths and Weaknesses

Make sure you get to know your team. By identifying strengths and weaknesses, you can make sure the right task is delegated to the right person.

Set expectations, set expectations, set expectations. Your team must know what you expect of them. If someone on your team is consistently not meeting expectations, then they may not be the best person for the task, and it may need to be reassigned.

Communicate

Communication is a crucial component when leading a project. You will want to make sure that you are frequently meeting with both your teams and stakeholders on a regular interval.

It is a good idea to setup weekly, bi-weekly, or monthly meetings and increase or decrease your intervals as needed. Make sure there is an agenda and that you make the meetings matter.

Send out emails as needed and be specific. Make sure your email as crucial information such as important dates/times, product information, names, etc.

Adjust Accordingly

You should anticipate issues as some always pop up. By understanding that there are always going to be some obstacles that arise when they do happen, you will be less stressed about it.

When problems arise, it is essential to get all key stakeholders and team members to the table to discuss a solution to the problem. Delegate someone to fix the issue, whether that is yourself or someone else, make sure an owner is assigned.

Things to Avoid

Manage Expectations

When communicating out to your team or to an individual regarding a project or a specific goal, it is crucial to communicate the expectations. If you lack details, it could cause the employee undue stress or misunderstand the request.

Use Reminders, Don't Rely on Memory Alone

Do not attempt to use your memory. Time slips away from us all. Emergencies come up, and people divide your attention. Make sure you are using reminders and set alarms on your calendar.

Build a Solid Team

Build a team based on experience and with those that have specific skill sets and not just on who is available. If you are only using "warm bodies," then it is likely that your team will not be highly proficient at the tasks at hand.

Communicate Properly

Poor communication with your team can cause major setbacks to the projects and could throw off the timeline. There is no excuse for failing to communicate with everyone.

Delegate

Don't do everything yourself! Make sure you are delegating out tasks as needed. You are supposed to be managing the project which is already taking up a lot of your time.

Don't Own Everything

Do not micromanage the team. Micromanaging your team can cause conflict with the owners of the tasks that have been given out. When you give the appropriate tasks to the right people, let them own the work.

20
Delegation

"Surround yourself with the best people you can find, delegate authority, and don't interfere as long as the policy you've decided upon is being carried out."

- *Ronald Reagan*

MAKE NO MISTAKE delegation is a powerful tool in your arsenal. By delegating tasks or projects to your team members, it empowers them and only makes them stronger. By taking on all the tasks or projects that come your way, you are adding undue stress on yourself. You are also doing a disservice to your team members and are stunting their growth.

As a leader, delegating can be one of the hardest things to do as it requires trust of those on your team to ensure the task is done correctly. Delegating can feel uncomfortable for some at first, especially for high performers. This may be a hurdle that you have to overcome so you can grow and become a stronger leader.

Fear of delegation is an illusion; break it, and you will have one of the greatest weapons to empower you and your team. Trust in yourself and your team will amaze you on how far they can reach their goals. The simple truth is that if everyone is involved in decision-making, they will be more committed to working to achieve making the ideal goal a reality.

The Importance of Delegating

The inability to delegate is one of the biggest problems of managers at all levels. Nevertheless, delegation is something that a leader will need to learn to do to be successful.

It's a simple fact that one person can't do everything. Trying to accomplish or micromanage too many tasks leads to burnout, poor quality, and missed deadlines, not to mention time management problems. Delegation is not a sign of weakness; it's a sign of leadership.

Reasons Why Leaders Fail to Delegate

1. Comfort Zone

Sometimes a leader feels more comfortable performing a task rather than doing other tasks. Perhaps they excelled at this task in a previous role. For others to grow, as a leader, we must let that go and focus on other tasks that need our attention.

2. Ease

A task or project may be easier done by one's self rather than having to teach, train, answer all of their questions and the employee may still get it wrong.

3. Control

Losing control is a big hurdle for most people, especially A-type personalities who generally want to be in control over everything. Letting someone else perform the task or job means losing a bit of control.

4. Perfection

The desire for perfection is most likely a part of the reason a leader is in their current role. Accepting anything less than perfection can be a strong reason why a leader may do it themselves. As the saying goes, "if it can't be done right the first time you might as well do it yourself." This can be a tough one to let go.

Reasons Why You Should Delegate

1. It Builds Trust

Being able to delegate effectively brings you and your employees closer and can build trust. It is essential to make sure you keep yourself available if they have any questions or concerns about the task or project you had given to them. By setting clear expectations and keeping the line of communication open, this can build a strong sense of trust between all parties.

2. Your Building A Strong Team

By providing your team with more tasks and duties to carry out, it allows the team to work on building their own skill sets that they may not have had the opportunity to do otherwise. This allows both the employee and the overall to grow. Remember that the leaders of the future have to come from somewhere and you can help with that.

3. Burnout

Attempting to do it all will eventually lead to burnout. While you're trying to 'do it all', you're killing your productivity, your speed to results and the quality of the works you're delivering.

4. Limiting Your Own Growth

Attempting to do it all will eventually lead to burnout. While you're trying to "do it all," you are killing your productivity, your speed to results, and the quality of the works you're delivering.

5. Team Workload Balance

Perhaps some of your employees are working 100 MPH, while others are spending too much time playing games and surfing the net. Ensuring your team has the appropriate workload balance shows that you are not only paying attention to everyone's daily activities but also makes sure everyone is doing their part.

6. Identify Better Solutions

Providing solutions to many problems may be one of the reasons why are you in a leadership role. However, getting feedback from your team is a great way to show them that their opinion matters. Besides, while you may feel you are right all of the time, sometimes there are better solutions to problems or angles you may not have seen.

7. Frees Up Your Time

You are in all likelihood spread thin as it is, and by delegating it allows you to focus and prioritize on other needs or projects. Effective delegation will enable you to maximize your own time, and it also can decrease any delays that may be caused by your inability to free up more time. As the saying goes, work smarter, not harder.

Vroom and Yetton's Leadership Decision Tree

As a leader, it can be challenging to understand when one should delegate, consult, or facilitate. Yale School of Management professor Victor Vroom and his colleagues Philip Yetton and Arthur Jago developed a decision-making tool. The Vroom and Yetton's leadership decision tree helps leaders determine how much involvement they should seek when making decisions.

Vroom and Yetton's model is somewhat complicated, but research results support the validity of the model. On average, leaders using the style recommended by the model tend to make more effective decisions compared with leaders using a method not supported by the model.

Although a little redundant at times, it can be particularly helpful in new or unusual situations. Practice using it, and you'll quickly get a feel for the right approach to take. Whether you're deciding a day-to-day issue or dealing with a more complex problem.

When taking a look at the model, it is crucial to understand each step, and there can be up to seven different steps to reach a conclusion.

Step One: Decision Significance

You will need to first ask yourself, is the quality of the decision high (H) or low (L)?

Step Two: Importance of Commitment

Next is team commitment of high importance or low importance for the decision?

Step Three: Leader Expertise

Does the leader have all the information needed to make a high-quality decision?

Step Four: Likelihood of Commitment

If the leader makes the decision alone, what is the likelihood that the employees would accept it?

Step Five: Goal Alignment

Are the employee goals aligned with organizational goals? Would the team support your decision if you made it alone?

Step Six: Group Expertise

Does the group have expertise in this decision-making area?
Step Seven: Team Competence

What is the ability of this particular team to solve the problem?

Now that you understand the steps make take a look at the next page and take those steps to determine which conclusion is the best for your situation.

Problem Statement	Decision Significance	Importance of Commitment	Leader Expertise	Likelihood of Commitment	Goal Alignment	Group Expertise	Team Competance	
H	H	H		H	-	-	-	Decide
			H	L	H	H	H	Facilitate
							L	
						L	-	Consult (Group)
					L	-	-	
			L	H	H	H	H	Delegate
							L	
						L	-	Consult (Individually)
					L	-	-	
				L	H	H	H	Facilitate
							L	
						L	-	Consult (Group)
					L	-	-	
	L	H	-	-	-	-	Decide
		L	-	H	H	H	Facilitate
						L	
					L	-	Consult (Individually)
				L	-	-	
L	H		H	-	-	-	Decide
			L	-	-	H	Delegate
						L	Facilitate
	L		-	-	-	-	Decide

Things to Avoid

Don't Give Up

Coaching your team members may be necessary, and some may not achieve the expected results on their first attempt. Allow your team to try again and make sure you are setting and managing expectations.

Micromanage

As discussed in several different chapters, micromanaging is one of the worst things a leader can do. You must step back and allow the employee to succeed or even fail. Failure is just another way for anyone to grow.

Don't Check Out

Just because you have delegated a task doesn't mean you can walk away entirely from the job or project. Make sure you are still engaged and remain informed in the project or task. If it is a project that is going to extend out for months, setting up a reoccurring meeting, such as a week, bi-weekly or monthly, is a great way to stay informed.

Don't Delegate Too Much

You mustn't overwhelm your team by delegating too much at one given time. There is such a thing as delegating too much, which can leave you disconnected. If at all possible delegate tasks or projects over time so they can better handle their workload.

Know Your Employees

You must know your employee's strengths and weaknesses before delegating a task. You want to make sure you are delegating to the right person. If you appoint a task or project to someone that does not have the right skill sets, you are just setting that person up for failure.

21
Negotiating

"Let us never negotiate out of fear. But let us never fear to negotiate."

- John F. Kennedy

THERE ARE TIMES IN ALL BUSINESSES as well as daily life where you must negotiate. Negotiating isn't always so easy, but it is an essential skill that you need to work on as a modern business professional. It is not uncommon for people to get caught in the moment and let their emotions take over.

Negotiating requires you to give and take. You should aim to create a courteous and constructive interaction that is a win-win for both parties. Ideally, a successful negotiation is where you can make concessions that mean little to you while giving something to the other party, that means a lot to them.

The Five Phases of Negotiation

A common way that parties deal with conflict is via negotiation. There are five phases of negotiation, which are described below. Each step is equally important to reach a mutual agreement successfully.

Phase One: Investigation

The first step in negotiation is an investigation or information gathering. Information gathering is a critical stage that is often ignored. Surprisingly, the first place to begin is with yourself: What are your goals for the negotiation? What do you want to achieve? What would you concede? What would you absolutely not concede?

During the negotiation, you'll inevitably be faced with making choices. It is best to know what you want so that in the heat of the moment you're able to make the best decision.

Phase Two: Determine Your BANTA

One important part of the investigation and planning phase is to determine your BATNA, which is an acronym that stands for the "best alternative to a negotiated agreement." Roger Fisher and William Ury coined this phrase in their book, *Getting to Yes: Negotiating Agreement Without Giving In.*

Thinking through your BATNA will help you decide whether to accept an offer you receive during the negotiation. You need to know what your alternatives are, and if you have various alternatives, you can look at the proposed deal more critically.

Phase Three: Presentation

The third phase of negotiation is presentation. In this phase, you assemble the information you've gathered in a way that supports your position. In a job hiring or salary negotiation situation, for instance, you can present facts that show what you've contributed to the organization in the past (or in a previous position), which in turn demonstrates your value.

Phase Four: Bargaining

During the bargaining phase, each party discusses its goals and seeks to agree. A natural part of this process is making concessions. Making a concession is not a sign of weakness—parties expect to give up some of their goals. Instead, concessions demonstrate cooperativeness and help move the negotiation toward its conclusion.

Phase Five: Closure

The closure phase is an integral part of the negotiations. At the close of a negotiation, you and the other party have either come to an agreement on the terms. Otherwise, one party has decided that the final offer is unacceptable and therefore must walk away.

Most negotiators assume that if their best offer has been rejected, there's nothing left to do. You made your best offer, and that's the best you can do. The savviest of negotiators, however, see the rejection as an opportunity to learn: "What would it have taken for us to reach an agreement?"

Sometimes, at the end of negotiations, it's clear why a deal was not reached. But if you're confused about why a deal did not happen, consider making a follow-up call. Even though you may not win the deal back in the end, you might learn something useful for future negotiations.

Negotiating Success

Focus On Agreements First

If you reach an impasse during negotiations, sometimes the best recourse is to agree that you disagree on those topics and then focus only on the ones on which you can reach an agreement. Summarize what you've agreed upon, so that everyone is on the same page, and leave out the points where you don't agree. Then take up those issues again in a different context, such as over dinner or coffee.

Be Patient

If you don't have a deadline by which an agreement needs to be reached, use that flexibility to your advantage. The other party may be forced by circumstances to agree to your terms, so if you can be patient, you may be able to get the best deal.

Deadlines

Research shows that negotiators are more likely to strike a deal by making more concessions and thinking more creatively as deadlines loom than at any other time in the negotiation process.

Silence is Golden

After you have made an offer, allow the other party to respond. Many people become uncomfortable with silence and feel like they need to say something. Wait and listen instead.

Understand Cultural Differences

Not understanding cultural differences is another common mistake made in negotiations. Some cultures have a higher or lower threshold for conflict. What works as a best practice in one culture may not work in a different culture.

Even the way that negotiations are viewed can differ across cultures. For example, Western cultures tend to think of negotiations as a business activity rather than a social activity, but in other cultures, the first step in negotiations is to develop a trusting relationship.

Mediation

In mediation, an outside third party (the mediator) enters the situation to assist the parties in reaching an agreement. The mediator can facilitate, suggest, and recommend, working with both parties to reach a solution but not representing either side. Instead, the mediator's role is to help the parties share feelings, air and verify facts, exchange perceptions, and work toward agreements.

Arbitration

In contrast to mediation, in which parties work with the mediator to arrive at a solution, in arbitration, the parties submit the dispute to the third-party arbitrator. It is the arbitrator who makes the final decision. The arbitrator is a neutral third party, but the decision rendered by the arbitrator is final (the decision is called the "award").

Arbitration-Mediation

It is common to see mediation followed by arbitration, but an alternative technique is to follow the arbitration with mediation. The format of this conflict resolution approach is to have both sides formally make their cases before an arbitrator. The arbitrator then makes a decision and places it in a sealed envelope. Following this, the two parties work through the mediation. If they are unable to reach an agreement on their own, the arbitration decision becomes binding.

Things to Avoid

Avoid Playing Hardball

A good rule of thumb is that hardball tactics should not be used because the negotiation is not likely to be the last time you will interact with the other party. Therefore, finding a way to make a deal that works for both sides is preferable. Otherwise, if you have the complete upper hand and use it to "destroy" the other party, it's likely that at a future date the other party will have the upper hand and will use it to retaliate mercilessly against you.

Remove Your Ego

Thinking only about yourself is a common mistake. People from the United States tend to fall into a self-serving bias in which they overinflate their worth and discount the worth of others. This can be a disadvantage during negotiations. Instead, think about why the other person would want to accept the deal. People aren't likely to take a deal that doesn't offer any benefit to them.

Having Unrealistic Expectations

Setting unrealistic expectations is a quick way to kill any negotiation. Setting expectations that are too far out of reach or for asking for way too much can easily insult the people you are attempting to come to terms with.

Failing to Negotiate / Accepting the First Offer

Researchers calculate that people who routinely negotiate salary increases will earn over $1 million more by retirement than people who accept an initial offer every time without asking for more. The good news is that it appears that it is possible to increase negotiation efforts and confidence by training people to use practical negotiation skills.

Becoming Too Emotional

Negotiations, by their very nature, are emotional. The findings regarding the outcomes of expressing anger during negotiations are mixed. Those who show anger negotiate worse deals than those who do not.

Not Letting Go of the Past

Those who were unable to negotiate some deal in previous negotiation situations tended to have lower outcomes than those who had successfully negotiated settlements in the past. The key to remember is that there is a tendency to let the past repeat itself. Being aware of this tendency allows you to overcome it.

Avoiding Conflict

Nothing ever good comes from avoiding conflict. Not dealing with an issue could very easily cause a problem to worsen over time. It is not uncommon for conflict to start small but become a disaster later on.

22
Networking

"If you want to go fast, go alone. If you want to far, go together."

- African Proverb

THERE ARE MANY REASONS why networking is so vital for your career. Being a connected manager or leader and improving your network skills can help you climb up that career ladder. Networking is not about just adding people to your social circles, or a popularity contest, it is about connecting with the right people.

Networking is also a great way to learn from not only the success of others but also what not to do. It is a great way to increase and expand your knowledge. There is an old saying that "iron sharpens iron" and networking around the right company is a great way to sharpen your skills.

There is another old saying, "it's not what you know; it's who you know." I disagree with the first half of that statement because making sure you are knowledgeable in your business is critical for a strong leader. However, increasing your network by growing your connections can open doors of opportunities that generally would either not exist or are difficult to open.

Network Properly

You want to make sure you are networking correctly. You must create a healthy business relationship with that person. It is very much about respect and being able to reciprocate resources and assets and that you are sharing them accordingly.

You need to be aware of a couple of areas that you should pay attention or focus on to build your network successfully.

Your Reputation

While networking is not about making friends, you need to give some thought to what other people think of you. While you may have been brought up and taught that it doesn't matter what people think of you, but it does when networking.

Once you decide on what type of leader you want others to see you as it will help you work towards that goal. An example of this would be that you may want to be recognized as a leader that is innovative or collaborative, or perhaps results-driven. Identify what you want to be known for and take actions to get you where you want to be.

Be Self-Aware

Remember that you have a brand and a reputation; you need to have a strong sense of self-awareness. Identify your strengths and use them. Identify your weaknesses and improve upon them.

Superior Performance

Be consistent with exceeding expectations, not just meeting expectations. If you are recognized as someone who is consistently exceeding expectations, then you will be known as someone that has high potential.

Understand You

It is essential to have a clear understanding of what you do, why you do it, who you do it for, and what you special for doing it. You would be surprised how many people struggle with explaining this. It is essential to not only know it but be able to articulate it.

Follow Through

Others need to view you as helpful and thoughtful. Helping others is a great way to have others identify you as dependable and resourceful, however, if you do not follow through on what you would say you would do you can quickly fall from grace and end up on their wrong side. If you are going to offer help, you must follow through and follow up with the individual that requested your assistance.

Your Alliances

A leader must make sure they have strong alliances. While some associations may be brief other may last throughout your career. Regardless of how long specific alliances last having the right partner and a strong partnership is a key corporate asset to have.

Business Objective

From a sales standpoint, it is essential to have a strong strategic alliance as it can help grow your customer base. If you are looking to expand it a new market having a strong partnership can strengthen your position and improve your business space to continue to grow.

Additional Resources

With all of the resources that you use daily to be successful in your business having a strong alliance that can help support your needs with additional resources is a great way to use to your advantage when needed. Keep in mind that you need to balance this and not take advantage of any assistance, and it is give and take.

Building a variety of alliances can help you in many different areas. To name a few examples of strategic relationships could be in marketing, technology, sales, supply chain, and vendor, etc.

Don't Compromise Your Values

There must be chemistry between you and your strategic alliances. Ensuring that you are working and aligning with like-minded individuals makes sure that your fundamental values are not compromised. When you compromise against your better judgment, your values can suffer.

Social Media

We are living in the age of social media. According to the Pew Research Center, 73% of all internet users use social networking sites. Whether we like it or not, many people live their lives online now. We have fewer expectations of privacy, and we are more likely to write about what we see than talk about it. Everything we do and say online has a broader audience.

Companies are paying attention to not only the applicant's social media presences but also to their employee's social media presence. Companies are consistently screening candidates based on their online presence. Online behavior that you demonstrate could not only prevent you from getting a job it can also cause you to lose your job.

Regardless of whether or not you agree that organizations should monitor employee behavior online, there are no laws that bar it. Social media is a great way to connect with employees, employers, and organizations and is an excellent way to network. It is important to remember that people have strong opinions, and your presence online could prevent you from making excellent contacts.

Keep your Brand Clean

Understand that you have a professional brand, one that potential employers may see when they try to research who you are social media. It is essential to keep it professional at all costs as some posts could paint a lousy picture.

Have you Googled yourself lately? If not, you probably should. Potential employers have begun searching the web as part of background checks, and you should be aware of what's out there about you. It's possible to set up automated reports with Google so that every time your name (or any other term) is mentioned on the web, you are alerted.

Things to Avoid

Avoid Negativity

While avoiding adverse situations are not always possible, it is a good habit to avoid keeping company with negative people. Surrounding yourself with positive and uplifting people will help you grow and thrive. Remember, "misery likes company."

Me, Myself and I

It can be easy to think only about your needs, but remember that networking is all about reciprocating. If you end up taking more than you give, you can find yourself alone. You'll see the more you return, the more likely someone will help you when you need a favor.

Don't Fake It

It is essential to the best version of yourself. However, it is also equally important to make sure you have honest interactions. You do not want to build yourself up artificially. Be the best version of yourself and be true to who you are.

Religion and Politics

Sure you have heard it before, and maybe you have been burned by this but never, ever, in a business environment bring up religion and politics unless you are sure you are speaking to like-minded individuals. You will wind up offending and alienating someone that could have been a staunch ally.

Avoid the Gossip

It's always good to be recognized as someone that has a pulse on the department or organization, or someone that is "in the know." However, you can easily be marked as the department gossip king or queen. Keep the gossip and banter to a minimum; otherwise, you may find yourself in an awkward position, and you run the risk of losing a reliable network contact.

23
Office Politics

"One of the penalties for refusing to participate in politics is that you end up being governed by your inferiors."

- *Plato*

OFFICE POLITICS EXISTS IN ALL ORGANIZATIONS, so it is essential to develop some political skill sets. Developing these skills can help prevent someone from taking advantage of you and also help you advance your career.

Being good at office politics in your organization includes knowing the right people to speak to, handling public put-downs well, making your work relevant, increasing your visibility, and moving projects along. It is vital to understand the political arena in your organization.

If you try to ignore office politics, there may be some consequences you may encounter. You must devise a strategy of how to navigate the political waters wherever you work successfully. Political proficiency is not a choice at work, but it's a necessity that can be improved at any point in your career.

Improve Office Politics Skills

There is no need to be afraid of office politics. There are a few excellent habits that you can master which all boil down to human communications and relationships.

Good politics involve advancing one's interests but not to the neglect of other people's rights or the organization's legitimate interests. Good politics include acceptable ways of getting recognition for your contributions, having your ideas taken seriously, and influencing what other people think and what decisions get made.

Build Your Connections

Networking is crucial, look beyond your immediate team, and cross the formal hierarchy in all directions – co-workers, managers, and executives. Don't be afraid of politically influential people. Instead, get to know them and build high-quality connections that avoid empty flattery.

Be friendly with everyone, but avoid aligning yourself too closely with one group or another. And, if you're considering a personal relationship at work, be certain to base it on consent, to avoid any suggestion of illegal or inappropriate influence, and to never break confidentiality.

Be Sincere

It is vital to be honest, open, and forthright. It is not enough to just be honest; sincerity is in the eye of the beholder. How honest you think you are is far less important than how honest other people think you are. When your integrity and values are at stake, do not fold. Everyone needs to see that you do have strong principles, and are not merely compliant with the whims of a political power center.

Identify the Cliques

Most workplaces will have informal groups and social cliques. It is essential to identify if these groups are based on friendship, mutual interest, or something else. Your best bet is to tread lightly when it comes to making alliances.

Cliques can have the illusion of safety in numbers; just remember this: Companies hire and fire individuals. Align yourself with people who are going to push you to be the best you can be and focus on how your efforts can help others.

Good leaders won't tolerate cliques and should create environments that foster community and inclusiveness. While healthy competition helps spur innovation in the workplace, cliques are truly more detrimental to your career than a benefit to it.

Develop Interpersonal Skills

When you build relationships with colleagues, you can also develop your interpersonal skills. Interpersonal skills can ultimately help you achieve social success in the workplace, as you may learn how to communicate effectively with teammates and superiors.

Your professional relationships can continue to develop based on practical interpersonal skills, so building your network and developing these skills can act as a revolving cycle of skill development and building friendships.

Be Socially Astute

Socially astute leaders tend to be conscious observers of others and social situations. They comprehend social interaction, and in social settings, they accurately interpret their behavior as well as that of others. They have strong powers of discernment and high self-awareness.

Things to Avoid

Don't Make it Personal

People tend to remember moments when they were humiliated or insulted. Even if you win this argument and get to feel good about it, for now, you'll pay the price later when you need help from this person. What goes around, comes around, especially at the workplace.

Don't Choose Sides

In office politics, it is possible to find yourself stuck in between two power figures who are at odds with each other. You find yourself being thrown around while they try to outwit each other and defend their position, all at the expense of you getting the job done. You can't get them to agree on a collective decision for a project, and neither of them wants to take ownership of issues; they're too afraid they'll get stabbed in the back for any mishaps.

By not taking sides, you'll help to direct conflict resolution in an objective manner. You'll also build trust with both parties. That'll help to keep the engagements constructive and focus on business objectives.

Avoiding Office Politics All Together

Office politics are unavoidable, whether you like it or not, handling the politics is part of what we do as leaders – in the sense that politics is the struggle for power and position in and across organizations. Politics is part of seeing organizations as they are – complex, living communities with histories, cultures, and dynamics of their own. It is also part of recognizing people as they are.

24
Next Steps

"The only way to get started is to quit talking and begin doing."

- *Walt Disney*

YOU SHOULD ALAWYS BE THINKING of your next steps and are continually be looking forward. Advancing your career falls solely on yourself. Unless you feel that the company that you work for is not the right fit for you it is best to set your focuses on an environment you are familiar with and start seeing what opportunities are available.

It doesn't matter what stage you're at in your career – the sooner you put your mind to it, the easier it will be to build a career you really want. The ideal career planning process is as well laid out and predictable one.

Areas of Focus

Identify Your Next Role

You should take a look at the landscape around you, and determine which role you would like for your next step. It provides you with a goal to achieve. You can start to devise a plan for what you need to do to meet that goal.

Find a Mentor

Identifying a mentor and start working closely with one. Finding a mentor is a great way to get feedback and identify some areas that you may need to focus. They will help you hone your skills, which in return will make you more competent at your job.

Find a Boss

This one is easier said than done; however, if you can find the right boss, it can work wonders for your career. Ideal bosses don't care about control as they help others achieve their objectives. They create an environment in which education and knowledge building is encouraged. Ideal bosses welcome ideas from their employees, which can bring out the best in people. Not only do great bosses inspire their employees, but they also believe in them.

One of the easiest ways to find a boss is if you are already working for a company and you can see the environment around you. If however, you are on the outside looking in, visit sites like glassdoor.com and linkedin.com to get perspective and feedback.

Education

Ensure that your education is current, you find that you need to update a certificate, get a different one, or finally get that diploma, and there is no better time than now to get started. Depending on the company, most offer educational reimbursement, use it to your advantage.

Identifying Your Replacement

From day one in your role, you should be identifying your replacement as it will take some time to get them up to speed.

Once you have identified your replacement, you then need to start making them your right-hand person. By keeping them close, providing those tasks that may be slightly outside of the job role will better prepare them for their next position and will give you a better idea on where their strengths and weaknesses are.

Keep your Resume Updated

Make sure you are always updating and developing your resume. Remember that you are marketing yourself, and if you do not provide a favorable impression, it could sink some of your chances. Avoid using templates, and if you are struggling with creating a resume, it is worth it to have a professional help work with you on one.

Practice Interviewing

It is a good habit when preparing for an interview to see if your mentor or peer can help you run through a few practice interviews. Interviews can be nerve-racking any getting some practice time before the event can calm the nerves and provide you a better chance at having a successful meeting.

Demonstrate a Strong Work Ethic

It is also good to demonstrate a strong work ethic. Showing your team that you have a strong work ethic indicates that you are committed to the goals and objectives. It also shows that you are striving to be successful in your work environment.

Things to Avoid

Don't Hold Yourself Back

You may feel pushed by your employer to take on the next role, or you may want to stay in your current position to get more exposure. There are times when you should leap to the next level as you may not know when the next opportunity will arise. Depending on your personality, you may never fully feel ready for your future role, but don't let that hold you back.

Sometimes we can be our own worst enemies. You need to be continually assessing yourself and try to figure out what you may want from your next role.

Watch Out For Bad Bosses

You must have the support of your boss. Having the support of your boss can either make or break your career. If you are working for a boss that doesn't feel like they are mentoring you and getting you ready for your next step, talk with them, and make sure they understand your needs. If they are still not supportive, see if there is another team you can join with a positive reputation.

Dead End Positions

There are a few signs that you may be in a dead-end job. It is essential to keep a lookout, and if you identify that you are in one, it is up to you to get yourself out of that situation.

1. Your manager can't identify a path for your growth within the company or if your manager has little or no interest in your career development.

2. The company's growth has slowed down. When a company's revenue slows down, there are generally fewer opportunities. You must be attending those financial meetings and paying attention to the reports.

Think About It

Don't just take a job because it was something that was offered to you. Your career moves need to be calculated and fully understood.

It's Not About Being Comfortable

Do not stay at a company simply because it is where you have always worked. I know we have all heard that the grass is not greener on the other side, but without deciding to look over the fence is just a wrong move. You could be the sole reason why your career has not progressed because you are comfortable where you are.

It's Not About The Money

If you haven't realized this already, it is not all about the money. You may be paid more in another role within your company or elsewhere. However, if you are not happy or do not believe in the work you do, then all the money in the world isn't going to make you happy. Most people learn this when it is too late, and they are stuck in a role they hate. This is something you need to be mindful of when looking to change positions.

Understand The "Why"

It is essential to understand why you want to make the change into a new role. Be sure you fully understand why you are looking to make a change or take the next steps.

Conclusion

"If your factions inspire others to dream more, learn more, do more and become more, you are a leader."

- *John Quincy Adams*

MANY ELEMENTS WERE COVERED in this book, which discussed certain areas that I would recommend to focus on as a leader. Many techniques have been covered and can provide you some insight into what a model leader should look like. Try to focus on and practice only a few items each week. Over a few months, you will find yourself becoming more influential in your role.

The techniques, models, and best practices that were covered are meant for you to take and make your own. We each have our styles, talents, strengths, and weakness that make us unique. I hope this information points you in the right direction to make you the best leader.

Keep in mind that only you have control over your path, and if you are driven enough and with the right team, you can and will move mountains.

Index

A

Accountability 12, 114
Affiliative 16
Anger 11, 35, 40, 121, 149, 180
Anxiety 37, 41, 84, 153
Arbitration 179
Arbitration-Mediation 179

B

Baby Boom Generation 134, 137, 138
Bargaining 149, 152, 177
Big Five 9
Bureaucratic Leadership 17

C

Cell Phone 48, 66
Change Management 142
Charismatic Leadership 17
Coaching 16, 91, 119, 173
Coercive 15
Controlling 33, 99, 160
Cultural Differences 178

D

Delegate, Delegation 12, 59, 165, 167, 168, 173
Democratic 16
Denial 149, 151
Depression 149, 153
Desk Phone 48

Difficult Employees 96
Discipline 14

E

Email 46, 47, 55, 94
Employee Conflict 103
Emotional Intelligence 33
Emotions 40, 109, 151
Employee Types 97
Empathy, Empathetic 11, 13, 42
Empowerment 12
Encouragement 26, 128
Engagement 73, 77
Evaluation 76, 81

F

Feedback 79, 80
Firing 122
Five Phases of Negotiation 175

G

Generation Alpha 137, 139
Generation X 134
Generation Y 135
Generation Z 136
Generations 132, 133
Group Development 84
Group Messaging 50

H

Hiring 69
Hiring Panel 69, 74
Honesty 13

Human Resources 119, 124

I

Improvement 80, 120
Instant Messaging 49
Intergroup Conflict 105
Interpersonal Conflict 104
Intrapersonal Conflict 104
Interview Grid 70
Interviewing 69, 194

L

Laissez-faire Leadership 17
Leading 160

M

Mediation 179
Meetings 62
Mentor 74, 138, 193
Mentoring Generations 138
Micromanaging, Micromanagement 27-33, 173
Millennial Generation 135
Mission 14
Multitasking 26

N

Negotiation 152, 175-181
Networking 182-187

O

Onboarding 72
One on One 50, 78

Organizational Behavior Modification 118
Organizing 160
Overextending 29

P

Pacesetting 16
Paperwork 52
Peer Panel 72
Performance 77-81
Performance Improvement Plan 120
Planning 159
P-O-L-C Framework 159
Procrastinate, Procrastinating 27, 61, 97
Project Management 158, 162
Public Speaking 51

R

Recognition 127-131
Reprimand 119
Reputation 183
Resistance 154
Responsibility 31, 60
Resume 194
Reward 79, 127-131, 145

S

Sadness 152
Self-Control 14
Servant Leadership 24-27
Seven Stages of Grief 149
Silent Generation 133
Social Media 185
Social Roles 88

T

Team Identity 91
Team Management 83-95
Team Roles 87
Team Strengths 163
Team Weaknesses 163
Teleconference 63
Terminating 123
Time Blocking 58
Time Management 56-61
Toxic Environment 110-116
Traditionalist Generation 133
Transactional Leadership 17
Transformational Leadership 17-19
Trust 31, 89, 90, 146, 147, 168

V

Vision 14, 16, 145
Visionary 16
Vroom and Yetton Decision Tree 169-172

W

Web Conference 63
Written Correction 117-122

www.ingramcontent.com/pod-product-compliance
Lightning Source LLC
Chambersburg PA
CBHW071358210526
45465CB00001B/160